FIND
BUILD
SELL

FIND
BUILD
SELL

FIND
BUILD
SELL

**HOW I TURNED A $100 BACKYARD BAR
INTO A $100 MILLION PUB EMPIRE**

STEPHEN J. HUNT

WILEY

First published in 2022 by John Wiley & Sons Australia, Ltd

42 McDougall St, Milton Qld 4064
Office also in Melbourne

Typeset in Plantin Std 10.5pt/14pt

© John Wiley & Sons Australia, Ltd 2022

The moral rights of the author have been asserted

ISBN: 978-0-730-39986-5

A catalogue record for this
book is available from the
National Library of Australia

Cover image: © MilenaKatzer/Getty Images
Cover design by Wiley

Disclaimer
The material in this publication is of the nature of general comment only, and does not represent professional advice. It is not intended to provide specific guidance for particular circumstances and it should not be relied on as the basis for any decision to take action or not take action on any matter which it covers. Readers should obtain professional advice where appropriate, before making any such decision. To the maximum extent permitted by law, the author and publisher disclaim all responsibility and liability to any person, arising directly or indirectly from any person taking or not taking action based on the information in this publication.

Some events, people and timeframes have been condensed, merged or truncated to keep the story rolling along.

SKYF80DA507-5010-4826-AD21-F38AE4066EFE_021122

This book is dedicated to my wife Fidelma and my children Holly, Suzie, Dermot, Aidan and Rory.

Contents

Contents

Acknowledgements

Writing this book has been a huge endeavour and one that could not have been possible without the support of my family and wider team. It's a representation of my journey through life (so far) and an opportunity to share the insights and experiences I have gleaned from that journey. I would like to shine a light on the many people who have walked this path with me, who have helped me and contributed a chapter of what has become the story of my life. I am grateful to you all.

Firstly, to my wife Fidelma and my children—Holly, Suzie, Dermot, Aidan and Rory—for your ongoing and unconditional love and support. I could not do what I do without your encouragement. You make it all worthwhile. (And to my two beautiful dogs, Dusty and Snoop, for helping me remember that at heart, I am a Hunter.)

To my mum Suzanne, my dad Peter and my siblings (David, Joanne, Phillip and Elizabeth) for the love and support you provided to me growing up, and a big thanks to my eldest brother, Dave, for being my rock and a constant voice of reason and sensibility.

To the Backyard Beer Tender: my childhood buddies, all legends in your own way, and in your own lunchtimes. You're a huge part of my life, then and now, as are your families. Thank you. In no particular order:

James Boyle	Jane Sandral
Daniel Wheeler	Katie Chad
Andrew Stevens	Belinda Driver
Stephen Duggan	Bridie O'Sullivan
Paul Hester	Sharnie Lofgren
Ben Taylor	Emma Hales
Neil Coyle	Penny Zatmury
Jon Farrell	Louise Malone
Gavin Yu	Michelle Jeffers
Grant Lyndon	Libby Ellis
Nick Russell	Lucinda Maloney
Simon Loughery	Jane Collins
David Sutton	Catherine Hamilton
Andrew Cairns	If I have forgotten anyone, I apologise.

To the Hunt Hospitality International (HHI) team: true champions in every way, for having my back and for your loyalty. You are my extended family. I hope I do as much for you as you have done for me:

Kris Gladwell	Corey Baker
Jason Archer	Wendy Berlin
Ricci-lee Wheeler	
Corey Park and Hannah Purdy	Terri Jones
Tony and Cat Jackson	Jeremy Cusack

My chief advisors:

Cath Antaw	Simon Rutherford
Andrew Wennerbom	Marin Kennedy
Alex Thompson	

To my investors and business partners past and present for your support. In no particular order:

Brent and Katia Penfold	Kathy Richardson
Tim Wearne	John Curnow
Michael Mitrovits	Graeme Cunningham
Annette Pulbrook	Gus Gilkison
Nick Wormald	

A special thank you to Greg Maitland for being my valued mentor; what you don't know about putting a deal together isn't worth knowing. Thank you.

To the Bayfield family, especially Wayne. You were great mentors who really taught me the importance of the community/pub relationship.

To the team at Westpac bank, Jeff Hurdis, Michelle Smith and Luba Finch, for being such honest and helpful bankers.

To James Brindley from Lion, Peter Filipovic from CUB, Michael Ritoli and Fred Jones from CUB Special Beverage, the team at LMG, especially Aidan Desmond and Amanda Williams for being such great supporters, the Australian Hotels Association (AHA) and in particular John Thorpe (RIP), Scott Leach, John Wheelan, John Green, Sean Morrissey and Phillip Ryan.

To the Hamilton Chamber of Commerce, Hunter Business Chamber and the Bar and Nightclub Show Las Vegas for your support.

To all the sporting teams that we support, and who support us:

The Wildfires (Hunter Rugby)

The Maitland Blacks Rugby Club

The Wahroonga Tigers

The Hornsby Lions

The Bogan Bulls (Nyngan).

And lastly, to Bernadette Schwerdt, for the time, effort and support you have put into helping bring my business story to life. Over countless conversations, hundreds of emails and thousands of words, you have helped me distil a rollicking and rowdy life into a book that I hope will be of value to many others. From when we first met, I knew you were the right person to help me tell my story, and my trust and instinct has been rewarded. Thank you for guiding me through this journey and for providing me with an outstanding learning experience. This book would not be the success it is without you.

And finally, a sincere and heartfelt thank you to every customer who has walked into one of our pubs. You are the reason we are here.

Introduction

My name is Hunt. Stephen Hunt. Clearly, my ancestors were hunters, and so am I. My name reflects perfectly what I do—so much so, I bought a dog, a German shorthaired pointer (Snoop, on the left), in honour of that ancestry. He is one of the best hunting dogs you can find. I bought him because he reminds me of who I am, and what I was destined to be.

Snoop, on the left, the best hunting dog you can find.

In short, I am a Hunter. I track down good pubs that have the potential to be great. I round up the team who can help me restore them to their former glory. I sniff out the best deals to maximise efficiencies. I then deliver them to my investors, and do it all again. I'll stop with the dog analogy ... you get the drift.

Hunt by name, hunt by nature

If you believe in the science of epigenetics, I am aptly named. Now epigenetics may sound like a depilatory tool you'd see for sale on The Shopping Channel, but it's the study of how behaviours and environment affect the way our genes work. Interestingly, a study discovered that 30 per cent of white men were more likely to match their career to their surname. (This is why we see Mr McBurney become a fire chief, Mr Brain become a neurosurgeon or Mr Soo Yoo a lawyer—all of whom are real people, by the way, according to the website 'boredpanda'.)

Is that luck, destiny, nature, nurture?

I don't know, and it doesn't matter. Whatever it is, I consider myself lucky to be The Pub Hunter. I've found myself here, at 48 years old, walking side by side with my wife and partner in life, Fidelma, our five children and a $100 million pub portfolio that continues to grow daily, delivering outstanding returns for my investors and life-changing opportunities for my employees and franchisees. I couldn't be happier with the way life turned out, but it wasn't all beer and skittles when I started out.

How I got started

I was a ginger-haired, fat-fingered, freckled-faced kid from suburban Sydney. I was also left-handed and had one kidney. What I did have going for me was that I was good with numbers and good with people. Those qualities have served me well. I now run Hunt Hospitality, a conglomerate that owns seven pubs up and down the east coast of Australia. We employ 350 staff and have won some of the most prestigious awards in the industry.

I started out washing dishes in pubs, and graduated to running them and, eventually, buying them. My modus operandi was simple: I'd choose poorly performing pubs, renovate, revalue and resell them for a higher price, repay the investors with an outstanding rate of return, and then do it all again. I got so good at buying pubs that friends, and then friends of friends, would say, 'Steve, can we be a part of this? Can I get in on the deal?', and I'd say, 'Sure', so I started to take on sophisticated, high-networth investors. I made them so much money, I became a private equity fund manager and started an investment fund, called The SJH Pub Fund. Top marks for creativity there, but it is what it is: a fund that owns, operates and manages a portfolio of successful pubs. I launched it in 2015 and it's been growing at a rate of 15.42 per cent with a cash return of 12.18 per cent per year since it started.

I'm not a trained accountant, but to manage such a complex investment portfolio, I had to become very, very good at reading numbers. And I did. I have my family to thank for that. My dad is an accountant, as are three of my four siblings, so I've been surrounded by numbers all my life. It wasn't unusual to talk about financial statements over breakfast, lines of credit over lunch and debt funding over dinner. My parents were ultra-conservative people, and they would have loved for me to become an accountant, but I had different plans. I took my passion for people and pubs and leveraged those talents to make a profit. I have found my strengths and made them work for me. When you find what you love and can make a buck from it, you'll never 'work' another day in your life.

The scent of a deal

I got my first 'scent' of a deal when I was four years old and was given a bucket of Lego for my birthday. I was playing with Luke, my next-door neighbour, and he said, 'Can I buy that bucket of Lego off you?' 'How much for?' I asked. 'Three dollars?' he said. This was a fortune for a little kid like me, and I fantasised about all the lollies I could buy with this unexpected windfall. I was about to say 'Sold!', when my mum pulled me aside and whispered, 'Stephen, think about it. You could sell the bucket to him for three dollars, or you could sell him the individual bricks for 50 cents a brick, and make 20 dollars. What would you prefer?' 'Can I charge him 70 cents a brick?' My entrepreneurial chops were on display, even then. 'That would be greedy, Stephen,' she said. 'And don't forget, Luke could go to the shops and buy them for less than that.'

In that moment, I discovered the principles of pricing structures and market forces. I owe my mother a great debt for teaching me, at such a young age, the essentials of entrepreneurship. I sealed the deal with Luke, headed down to the shops and filled my pockets with cobblers and chocolate bullets.

My father taught me my second lesson. When I was 10, we took a family trip to Hong Kong. We lined up at the money exchange counter to buy some Hong Kong currency. I watched my dad hand over the money to buy the notes, and a moment before the money changed hands, the exchange rate went up, and in the blink of an eye, we were given $200 more than if we had bought it a few seconds earlier. In that moment, I learned that timing is everything: a critical element when buying and selling a business.

The $100 backyard bar

I have to be honest. I didn't set out to become a publican. Growing up in a middle-class suburban home with two rugby-loving brothers (and two equally sporty sisters), I was a sports-mad jock with a grand goal to play rugby for Australia. I did make several representative rugby union and league teams, represented my school in 11 different sports and was captain of the swimming team. Unfortunately, however, my talent did not quite match my ambitions. As a result, I had to find another career. But as a 17 year old, fresh out of school, I had no idea what I wanted to do. I was too busy mucking around with my mates, playing footy, drinking beer and having fun. Which is kind of how my business began. As they say, from little things big things grow. My pub empire started as a very small operation: it started in my backyard.

When I was 17 years old, my dad bought a massive BBQ and installed it down the back of the yard. It was a concrete monstrosity with a built-in chimney, removeable grills, cast-iron hotplates and more. He decked out the area with second-hand armchairs, eskies, a tarpaulin tent to keep out the rain, a tape deck and speakers so we could listen to music, and a string of party lights dripping off the trees so we didn't trip over in the dark.

He must have wanted us out of the house. It worked.

I spent most of my weekends down there, hanging out with my high-school buddies. I'd invite them all over after the footy, we'd get a few girls from school to come along and before you knew it, every teenager in the street would be popping over to see what the noise was all about. Everyone was welcome — even the teachers. It wasn't unusual on some weekends to have 100+ people down the back of the yard, partying away, with me at the helm. My parties got so popular, I rallied my mates to help me manage the logistics. One took care of the food, the other bought the grog, another manned the gate to deter any undesirables from dropping in. We were a well-oiled team.

One night we ran short of beers so my mate said, 'Just charge them $2 for the beer you've got left in the esky' — so I did. I took that money, went down to the pub, bought more beers, came back, sold those and made $100! I was stoked. Not only had I made a few bucks, I had enabled the party to carry on late into the night. I looked around at the faces of my friends laughing, joking, dancing, drinking: I could see the joy they were experiencing, feel the happiness they were exuding, and it was exhilarating. I had brought together this disparate group of people from many walks of life, and they were all having a great time because of me. I was having a ball too, but what I really enjoyed was watching other people have a good time. In that moment, my mate Paul turned to me and he said, 'Steve, I reckon you should do this for a living'.

'So do I, mate. So do I.'

And now I do.

This is my story.

What's this book about?

Success leaves clues. I've written this book so you can stand on the shoulders of those who have gone before and fast track your success; so you can minimise errors, maximise opportunities and get cracking on your business idea as soon as possible. When I set out on this journey 30 years ago, I had no idea what I was doing or where it would lead. I do now and it's been a helluva ride. This book is the step-by-step guide to how I did it—a blueprint of sorts—so that you have the tools you need to find, build and sell the business of your dreams. Rip in.

Find

What do you love? What are you good at? What does the market want? 'Find' the intersection of these three critical questions and you've got the foundations of a successful business. 'Find' is about identifying the right business idea for you, be it a new or existing entity, and finding the right team of people who can help you bring that idea to life. It's about finding the principles and values underpinning your entrepreneurial vision that will guide your very decision. It's about finding your strengths (and your weaknesses) so you can do more of what you love, and less of what you don't. It's about finding time to focus on what's important, and what's not, and knowing how to tell the difference. It's about finding the tools to curb anxiety, conquer worry and build resilience so you can stay the distance.

Build

Do you run the business, or does it run you? Are you working in it, or on it? 'Build' is about taking the business you've bought (or created) and applying robust systems, procedures and processes so that you can automate the business without duplicating effort or reinventing the wheel. It's about how to 'build' your confidence, manage risk and create an intrapreneurial culture that answers the fundamental questions of 'Why are you in business?' 'What do you stand for?' and 'Who do you want to be?' It's about building systems that minimise conflict, improve productivity and maximise profits.

Sell

Do you have an exit strategy for the business? Do you want to sell it, stay with it or list it? What's the end goal? 'Sell' is about building upon what you've created and maximising opportunities. It's about how to 'sell' yourself, your vision and your story to attract investors and partners who can help you realise your ambitions. It's about how to evaluate investment opportunities, source venture capital, negotiate the deal, prepare the business plan, pitch to investors and choose the right advisors.

Who is this book for?

You may not want to own a pub, but you can learn a lot of lessons from someone like me who has. Why? Because I live in the real world of business. I live in a world where my business lives and dies by the sword of selling a service at a profit that sustains me, my staff and my investors. If I don't sell something, to someone, today and every day, I fail. It's as simple as that. Unlike those in the tech sector and start-up land (and good luck to them, by the way), I don't have the luxury of telling investors, 'Invest in this obscure, untested, untried software that one day, somehow, will make you an absolute fortune. We don't have any sales, customers, traction, history or profit yet, but trust me, one day, we will!'

No. That's not the world I live in, and chances are, it's not the world you live in either. You're a small-business owner, working hard to chase your dream and turn your idea into a profitable enterprise. You get up early, stay back late, work like crazy in between, get home, say 'hi' to your family, collapse and then get up and do it all again the next day. In short, you're exhausted, you're overwhelmed and you want to do things differently.

You want to enjoy what you do, grow the business without going into debt, make it more profitable, do more with less and get smarter about the way you manage yourself, your team, your energy, your time and your money. You want to attract more, better customers who can afford what you offer: who love what you do and aren't afraid to tell the world about it.

You don't want to be a billionaire, or maybe even a millionaire. You just want to have a thriving business that lets you do what you want to do, that pays you for a job well done; you want a business that runs without needing you to do everything; that has systems and procedures in place that ensure you know what's going on even when you're not there; that runs like clockwork so you can get on with working *on* the business, instead of *in* the business; that lets you get back to being with your family, taking a holiday now and then and sleeping soundly at night—without waking at 3 am worrying about cash flow, deal flow or work flow.

What problem does this book solve?

I've been running pubs since I was 18 and I've learned a few things along the way, and how to build a multimillion-dollar, multi-venue corporation is one of them. Through trial and error, I've discovered a blueprint for business success, and the best part is, my blueprint works for any business. Whether you're a hairdresser, stockbroker, fashion designer or car dealer, this system will work for you too.

If you live in the real world, like I do, and you'd like to learn how you can turn your passion into profit, do what you love and get paid handsomely to do so (so that you never have to work in a job you hate because the work you do is what you were born to do), this is the book for you.

There's never been a better time to make a change. If ever you were going to do something differently, the time is now. Don't waste another minute doing something you don't want to do, for a boss or company you neither like nor respect, for a wage or conditions that don't reflect your true worth, talent and potential. Don't be an armchair critic. Get out there, throw your hat in the ring and get cracking. After all, if a left-handed, one kidney-ed, ginger-haired kid from the back blocks of Sydney can do it, so can you.

Welcome to my world. The real world. Let's get started.

Part I
FIND

You've got an idea and found your passion and now you want to set up the rules of engagement for how you'll take on staff, customers and investors. So let's work out your strengths, identify your blind spots and help you develop the courage to try to step out of your comfort zone and develop strategies for mitigating the risks if you fail.

It's now time to discover the importance of finding time to focus on what matters, like being in the right room and taking time to learn and do the little things right.

Let's go!

CHAPTER 1
Find your passion

I've got seven pubs worth over $100 million. Saying it like that makes it sound like it was easy to achieve. It wasn't. It's taken me 30 years to learn the formula for how to find, build and scale a bricks and mortar business. In the early days, I made many mistakes. In fact, I made so many I nearly went bankrupt before I had even begun.

I started out making $100 at my backyard bar and gradually worked my way up, managing bars all over Sydney, London and Europe, working for some of the biggest and best names in the business. I was a sponge, absorbing everything around me, just waiting for that day when I could do it for myself and be my own boss.

My opportunity came, funnily enough, when I was sitting in a bar. What I'm about to tell you sounds like a plot from a Hollywood movie, but I can assure you that everything that happened was very real. I'm revealing the story here so that (hopefully) you can avoid repeating the rookie errors I made.

How *not* to buy a pub

It was 2015. I was 42. I was living in the Hunter Valley, New South Wales with my wife and children. By sheer good luck (and some good timing), I found myself with $400000 from the lucrative sale of a Sydney residence. I had already had a few good wins under my belt from residential property (I once owned a property for six weeks and made 18 per cent on the sale), so I was feeling on top of the world and, to put it quite bluntly, thought my shit didn't stink.

As it happens, my local bar — The Rutherford, two hours north of Sydney — was up for sale. I'd spent many a night in this bar and thought, 'Maybe this is the business opportunity I've been looking for?' It had a good vibe, a terrific location, minimal competition and great community support. After a few more days of mulling it over (and, it must be said, a few more drinks in that bar), I thought, 'Yep! This is a winner. I'm going to buy this bar!'

The Rutherford Hotel. The bar that set the wheels in motion.

I'd been managing pubs for 20 years as a CEO and general manager, but I'd never sought investors to assist with the funding of them. This would be an entirely different endeavour. But my time was here. This was a wonderful opportunity and I knew I could make it a success.

The next day, I contacted the hotel broker who was selling the pub.

'How much are you asking for The Rutherford on the New England Highway?' I asked.

'$4.2 million,' he said.

'Sounds reasonable,' I said, privately thinking I had no hope in hell of finding that much money, but I wanted to give it a red-hot crack so I went to my accountant, told her about the deal and to my surprise and delight, she said, 'Count me in. I'll invest $400 000 right now'. Well, that was a good start, I thought.

With the help of a few other friends, I found another $200 000, so with my $400 000 from the property sale and my accountant's $400 000 contribution, I now had $1 million dollars to kick start my venture.

I went to the bank and told them what I needed to buy this bar. The first one said 'no', and so did the second and third. The fourth one, however, said 'yes' to my request, so now I had a total of $3.73 million. Brilliant. It was a struggle to get that bank to have faith in me, but having run many pubs in the past, they could see I knew what I was doing.

Now I just needed to raise $1 million to complete the purchase. 'Piece of cake', I thought.

Just $1 million to go

I made a list of the top 10 people I thought would be interested (the classic three Fs: family, friends and foes). I went from one house to the next, pitching the idea to them in their kitchens and loungerooms, and guess what? All 10 of them said, 'Yes!' They said, 'Steve, we would love to be part of this and can't wait to get started. Just let us know when you need the $100 000, and we are in!'

'How easy was this?' I said to myself. 'I should have done this years ago!'

I now had the final million I needed to complete the deal. I went back to the hotel broker, signed the contract and bought the bar! Happy days. I was beyond excited. I celebrated all week with my family and mates, thrilled to be embarking on this exciting venture.

I followed up with the 10 investors to tie up the loose ends and confirm the paperwork. I sent them the information memorandum (more about information memorandums in chapter 8), which outlined the deal, the bank account details and the application forms for signing, and they all said, 'Yeah, sure thing Steve, no problem. We're right there with you. The money's coming'.

Except the money didn't come.

I checked my account every day to see if their funds had been deposited. Nothing there. I waited another week. Still no sign. I rang them all again. For some strange reason, none of them answered their phone. I sent them an email. Still no response. I went to their home and knocked on their door. No answer. That's strange, I thought. They were so keen a week ago.

I wasn't worried. I had a few more Fs to chase up and felt confident I could come up with the funds, but those phone calls, emails and door knocks also went unanswered.

The settlement date loomed. I was still $1 million in the hole and there was no sign of any new investors coming to this party any time soon. What had seemed like an exciting adventure and simple endeavour four weeks ago had become a bit of a nightmare.

What happened to my investors?

I was worried now; worried enough to start talking to lawyers to see if I could extricate myself from this mess I had created. I asked them two key questions: can I get out of this contract without penalty, and if not, how bad will it be?

Their answers were pretty clear cut. No, and very bad. Not the answers I was hoping for.

I decided to take the personal route and rely on my charm and sincerity to see if that would work. I rang the hotel broker who sold me the bar and I said, 'Mate, you know that money that I was going to raise to buy the bar with? Well, turns out I've fallen short as a key investor has pulled out. I don't suppose we could get an extension on the settlement?

'Ah, I don't think so,' was his response. Not the response I was looking for. He said, 'I recommend you have a chat with the actual owner of the bar. He may be more accommodating than me'.

I jumped in the car, drove like a mad man, barged into his office and said, 'I really want this bar, but I just need a bit more time. Can you give me an extension?'

He said, 'I'll think about it and get back to you'.

I waited by the phone like a love-sick teenager, desperate for his call.

He didn't call.

Another day went by. No answer. Then another day. Still no call. I was now completely stressed out, on tenterhooks, waiting for an answer. My options were looking very grim. *If I can't come up with the rest of the money, I forfeit the deposit, a very hefty $420 000, and will be sued for the rest of it too — an extremely hefty $4 million.*

Finally, with two days to go before settlement, the bar owner rang me and said, 'With regards to your request to extend the time frame, I have one word for you. No'.

The next day, I got a call from his lawyers. They said, 'If you don't come up with the money, we will sue you for non-completion', which is a fancy way of saying, 'If you don't come up with the cash, we'll sue your arse off'.

I felt sick. My chest tightened, my stomach clenched, my heart raced. This was definitely not the response I was hoping for. My negative self-talk went into overdrive. *How did I get myself into this mess? What was I thinking? If only…* were the words that danced around my head.

If only I'd got those investment guarantees in writing.

If only I had more time before settlement.

I cursed those who had let me down, but mostly, I cursed myself for counting my chickens before they had hatched; for making assumptions, and being impetuous. These qualities had mostly served me well in the past, but not this time. Now they could cost me everything I had worked for, and more. But it was my own fault, and I had no-one to blame but myself. I was in the shit and I had to find a way out. If I couldn't, I'd lose all my assets: my house, my super, my savings. I had five children to support so it was no joke. I was about to lose everything.

Time is running out

I now had less than 24 hours to come up with a million dollars and I had zero prospects of achieving that. So I turned to the only figure I could think of: St Francis, the patron saint for lost causes; the saint all lapsed Catholics turn to when they've lost all hope. I said, 'St Francis, get me out of this pickle and I promise I will go to mass every Sunday. I'll bring the kids too; heck, I'll even take them to Confession!'

St Francis promptly told me to get off my arse and contact someone who actually had the power to help me, so I went back to the original 10 who had expressed interest and said, 'Look, I just need to know if you're in or out. I don't mind which way you go (I did), but I just need an answer'. 'We're out,' they said. Well, at least I knew where I stood.

I said, 'Okay, you may not want to invest, but do you have any friends who may want to invest?' And fortunately, they did. They were probably just trying to fob me off to get me to stop bugging them, but to my great relief, they gave me 10 names to follow up.

I rang them all. Seven said, 'Thanks, but no'. Three said, 'Maybe, let's talk'. Bingo! All was not lost. I had three shots to raise a million dollars.

I was on a mission.

I did not waste time sleeping that night (I couldn't sleep anyway), so at 3 am I got up and went for a jog in the dark. As I jogged along that cold, lonely street, I reflected on how I had got myself into this stressful situation, and I beat myself up for being so naïve. But I realised that the only person who could turn this around was me, and giving up was not in my nature. Even when I played football and we were losing 50 to 1, I always believed we could turn it around. This was no different. With each step, I reiterated the beliefs that had sustained me in darker times than this: *There is always a way. You can do this. Don't give up.*

How to raise $1 million in a day

Later that morning, I drove the 200 kilometres from my home in the Hunter Valley to Sydney for my final round of investor meetings. I had three appointments booked and each of them had to say 'yes' if I was to avoid being bankrupted.

My first meeting was with two parents from my son's school, a successful power couple whom I liked and respected. I took them through the information memorandum, answered all their questions and tried to keep the panic from rising in my voice. At the end of my presentation, he sat back, put his arms behind his head, looked me in the eye and said, 'I'm in'. 'How much for?' I asked. '$200 000,' he said.

I could have kissed him (I didn't). I was elated. Finally, someone could see the vision I had and was willing to back me! As I packed up my bag to move onto my next investor meeting, he said, 'Who else is investing in this?' I told him who I had lined up next, and out of nowhere he said, 'Make it $250 000'.

Once I was out of eyesight, I wiped the sweat from my brow, metaphorically high-fived myself and drove like crazy to my next meeting. I was so nervous I went to the wrong address, but fortunately I had left enough time and got there on time. This meeting was with two super-experienced business owners and investors. They'd just sold another business a few weeks earlier and were cashed up, but they were no pushovers. I went through the pitch, showed them the projections and watched them like a hawk to gauge their reactions. They were unmoved, saying, 'We'll think about it and let you know in a few days'.

I didn't have a few days but couldn't tell them that for fear they'd smell my desperation and pull out, and besides, no-one likes to think they're the last cab off the rank.

I was devastated. I was so close. The clock was ticking. It was 2 pm. I had until 5 pm before settlement was due.

One of the guys walked me back to my car in the parking lot. I felt sick at how close I had come to getting these investors over the line. I had to do something to see if I could fast track their decision. I wound down the car window and said, 'Mate, I don't mean to be rude, but just out of interest, if you were to invest, how much would it be for?'

He looked at me and said, 'We'd invest $300 000. Each'. And then, with a few words that would change my life, he said, 'It seems like you need an answer sooner rather than later, so consider it a done deal'.

I could have kissed him too (I didn't). But again, I was ecstatic! I now had $850 000 in the kitty and one meeting to go to raise the last $150 000. It was 4 pm. One hour to go before settlement. Time was against me. I practically ran to the other meeting, which was, fortunately, just around the corner.

There were three men at this meeting: a potential investor and two fund managers.

I hadn't met this investor before, but from the moment we sat down, we hit it off. Turns out, we grew up in the same neighbourhood, he knew my family and we had common friends. Before I had even finished my pitch, he said, 'Steve, I've heard enough. I'm in for $50 000'. My heart sank. I was grateful for him opting in, but it still left me $100 000 short.

I stood up, smiled and shook their hands, trying to act enthusiastic. But I knew I was cactus because I hadn't raised the full amount. My time was up. I had to concede defeat. Just as I was about to walk out the door, the two fund managers stopped me and said, 'Do you have room for more?' Trying to look cool, calm and collected, I said, 'Possibly. How much are you looking to invest?' They said, '$50 000. Each'.

My brain made the quick calculation. You bloody beauty! I had done it! I had raised $1 million in eight hours and in the process saved my house, my savings and the future of my family.

I went back to the hotel broker, handed over the cheque at 4.50 pm and took proud possession of my bar. Other than the birth of my children, this was one of the proudest moments of my life. I had come very close to losing everything. I was on my way. I had prevailed. Life was never going to be the same again.

I learned many a lesson from this experience, most of them about what not to do. For a start, don't take people at their word, don't assume anything before you have it in writing and most importantly, don't buy a bar before you have the money in the bank.

How to find your passion

Everything happens at the pub. It's where the locals go to celebrate, commiserate, congratulate and communicate, and I love being at the centre of what's happening. I'm the guy at the side, gently nudging the proceedings along by tweaking the dials to create the right mood and atmosphere — the music, food, lights, colours, scents, décor, drinks — these are the levers that bring a party to life. That's what I do. And I bloody love it.

I've been doing it since I launched my backyard bar and I've been in the industry ever since. I don't know it all, but I know what it takes to succeed. Fortunately, my passion for pubs connects with my ability to turn a profit, but it's worth remembering this: it's one thing to have a passion for a business idea. It's quite another to make it profitable, and just because you like something doesn't mean you can make money from it. You might enjoy making pottery, but it doesn't mean you should build a business around it. Do you like the business of selling pottery, or do you just like making pottery? It's an important distinction to make because not everything you love is commercially viable. There's a lot that goes into running a business, much of which you may not like, be good at or know how to do. So you need to ask yourself some questions to find a passion that you can cash in on.

5 questions to ask yourself when choosing a business idea

1. *Is what you love relevant to other people?* Do people love what you have? I happen to love pubs, and people love pubs, so it's a good match. People need to want what you have.

2. *Will the customer pay you for what you have?* What problem do you solve? You'll get paid if you help people solve their problem. In my world, people will always pay for a pint, a parma, a punt or a party.

3. *If everyone else is already doing it, can you do it differently?* Beware of unwarranted optimism—that is, believing that just because you offer it, people will come. You need to have a clear point of difference and the ability to communicate that to a market who value that difference.

4. *Can you find a customer?* You don't need hundreds of customers to validate your business idea. You need one. The minute someone pays you for what you have (at market rates) you have a business idea worth exploring.

5. *Is it profitable?* Selling it for a fee is one thing. Making a profit is another. If it costs so much to make it that you can't make a profit, you need to find a cheaper way to make it or find a different business model.

If you don't want to lose money (like I nearly did) by making a poor decision, think carefully before you buy or launch a business. I didn't, and I nearly lost my entire life's savings. Fortunately, I was able to turn it around, but many can't, or don't, and what starts out as exciting can quickly become overwhelming or downright terrifying. Don't let this happen to you.

BEWARE OF UNWARRANTED OPTIMISM

Hope is not a marketing strategy. Neither is optimism, especially when it's unwarranted.

Knowing how to assess an opportunity is key, and doing your due diligence is the secret to getting that assessment right. Even if you're totally besotted with an opportunity, you need to look at it through an objective lens, and see if from all points of view, to see if the deal stacks up. Being prepared to walk away from it is also critical. It takes a lot of guts for the head to overrule the heart, but when it comes to buying and investing, there's no room for emotion.

For example, there's a coffee shop on a corner near me. It's the third coffee shop in two years to take a lease at that location. The previous two went out of business. From what I can see, this one will too because it's exactly the same as the two that went before it. The name is different, the décor is different and the people are different, but for all intents and purposes, it's a coffee shop just like the others. So, you have to ask the question: if the other two failed, why do these new owners think they will succeed?

I can tell you why: it's because the new owners have an unwarranted optimism about their likelihood of success—a misplaced sense of enthusiasm that, this time, it'll be different—because they think they are better operators, better coffee makers or just…better. I hope they are, but I doubt it.

This excitement at 'what could be' obfuscates the reality of 'what is'. They ignore the obvious warning signs about what could go wrong. In this case, the café has no atmosphere, no parking and no foot traffic. I hope for their sake this time something will be different.

The easiest way to determine what you should build, or buy, a business around is by asking these three questions:

- What do I love doing?

- Do people need it?

- Will people pay for it?

Find the overlap in those three questions and you've found the business to pursue.

Summing up ...

1. Don't count your chickens before they hatch.

2. Don't get cocky.

3. If someone says 'no' to an investment, ask if they know of anyone who could be interested.

4. Get your accountant and lawyer to look over all contracts before you sign anything.

5. Don't confuse your passion for making something with your ability to sell it or market it.

6. Beware of unwarranted optimism. Do your due diligence before you buy a business or invest in one.

CHAPTER 2
Find your feet

Waste no more time arguing about what a good man should be. Be one.
Marcus Aurelius

I saw Steven Spielberg interviewed once. He was launching a new blockbuster film and the interviewer asked him, 'How do you deal with the pressure of managing such big budgets, and how can you bolster your chances of having a best-selling movie?'

He said, 'Ninety-nine per cent of a film's success is in the casting. If I get that right, the rest will take care of itself'.

Don't let them in

It's the same with pubs, or any business for that matter. 'Casting' is critical to success. In other words, who we 'let in', be they a patron, an employee, an investor or a supplier, dramatically impacts our ability to be successful, because everyone we 'let in' brings with them a whole bunch of baggage that can very quickly become ours.

Running a hospitality business like a pub is quite different from running a law firm, a factory or a furniture store, in that most of those businesses don't have 10 000 strangers streaming through their doors each week to eat, meet and greet who treat the place as an extension of their loungeroom. That kind of 'random fun factor' of never knowing who or how many people will come in creates a level of unpredictability that means we have to employ robust procedures to ensure that we don't let the wrong people in.

This is tricky and somewhat counterintuitive because as a publican, I'm in the business of letting *everybody* in. In fact, the more we let in, the better, so working out who to let in and who to keep out is a delicate balancing act. Do we have a strategy for managing this? Yes. It's very simple. It's called 'don't let them in' in the first place.

The reason this is so important is because I know that once someone is on the premises, it becomes very difficult to get them off the premises, so I work very hard to ensure that they don't even get past the front door. Sure, a few rock stars (real and imagined) can dazzle us with their brilliance and get in the side door causing a few upsets, but for the most part, if we work hard to not let them in to begin with, the time and effort taken to remove them is minimised.

That's why we have bouncers (or security guards, as we now like to call them) and I employ a lot of them these days. They are a critical factor in helping me keep the undesirables out and taking care of the good people who are already in. A good bouncer is worth their weight in gold! And their presence can save lives. Here's how one saved mine.

WHY I LOVE BOUNCERS

One of my pubs—The Kent Hotel in Hamilton, New South Wales, two hours north of Sydney—is a popular venue for partygoers. Prior to me owning it, it was renowned for being a place where people came to sort out their 'disputes'. I definitely didn't want that to be the case moving forward, so I invited the licensing sergeant from the local police station to come in and give me an assessment of what we needed to do to minimise the violence.

'How bad does the brawling get here?' I asked him.

'Put it this way,' he said. 'There's been 52 assaults in the past 12 months, which is one a week, which makes it the most violent pub in New South Wales. Congratulations!' he said.

'Thanks,' I said. 'What do you recommend we do to minimise the violence happening in this building?'

'Move the building,' he said.

He wasn't joking.

I relish a challenge, so I was super pumped at having the opportunity to turn this place around. I met with my newly acquired team and said, 'Okay everyone! Fresh start. We're going to clean this place up. We're going to change everything—the menu, the music, the décor, the staff, the security—everything. And most importantly, we're going to change who we let in. From now on, if you see any troublemakers heading for the entrance, tell me who they are, point them out and we'll bar them from entering'.

Two days later, Matt, the barman, came over and said, 'Steve, there's a guy called Craig coming down the street, and he's headed for our hotel. He's bad news'.

'In what way?'

'He's aggressive, abuses staff and breaks shit.' Great. Just what I needed on a Saturday morning.

Sure enough, a few moments later, this six-foot-four bruiser of a body builder in double denim (he may have been big, but he sure had no dress sense) arrived at the door. Being 11 am on a Saturday, I only had Matt on staff.

Craig ambled up the steps to the entrance, peered down through blood-shot eyes and sneered, 'Out of my way'.

I stuck my hand out and said, 'G'day mate. My name's Steve. I'm the new owner of the pub'. He brushed my hand aside and pushed past me to get inside.

(continued)

'Hey, hey buddy, slow down a little,' I said.

'Get the fuck out of my way,' he said.

'Well, mate, if you're not going to shake my hand and be civil before you come into my pub, I'm afraid I can't let you come in.'

He stood back, looked me up and down and said calmly, in a low voice, 'Fine. I'll just go and get my gun and come back and shoot you and everyone in your fuckin' pub, then'.

Any normal person would take a threat like this seriously, but I had worked in pubs far worse than this, so I just smiled and said, 'Well mate, I knock off at 5 pm so make sure you come back by then, okay?'

He looked at me with his mad-dog eyes, and walked off.

Whoo! I thought. *That was easier than I thought.* I went back inside, poured a few beers and got on with my day.

An hour later, Matt rushed over to me, his brow furrowed.

'Hey boss, we've got trouble. He's back.'

'Not Craig?'

'Yep.'

'Shit.'

Fortunately Alex, one of my off-duty security guards, had popped in to check his roster for the week. I pulled him aside and explained what had happened.

We stationed ourselves at the entrance, arms crossed, waiting.

Craig pushed past me to get in. I placed my hand firmly on his chest.

'Mate, there's a dozen bars in the area. Choose another one,' I said.

'I don't want to choose another one. I'm coming in here,' he said.

'I'm sorry mate,' I said, 'but I've already made it clear to you that you're not welcome here'.

'I'm coming in here!' he said, and then grabbed me by the shoulders and went to head butt me. I dodged at the right moment, but he kicked my legs out from under me and before I knew it, I was on the ground with this hulk of a man lining up to kick me straight in the temple.

I grabbed the leg he was about to kick me with, twisted it and upended him. Now we were both on the ground, wrestling. Alex leaned down, grabbed the guy by the back of his jacket, pulled him up and threw him up against the wall. Craig kept swinging his fists, cursing like a drunken sailor. As he went to throw another punch, his jacket flew open and what did we see tucked inside his belt? A .44 magnum revolver. It looked real — very real — mainly because it was.

Alex yelled out, 'He's got a gun!' We threw him to the ground, grabbed the gun from his belt and held him to the ground until the police arrived. As the police left, one of them turned to me and said, 'You guys were lucky. This guy just got out of prison'.

'What did he do to get in?' I asked.

'He shot a man.'

A cold shiver ran down my spine. This guy wasn't mucking around and those threats he made were real.

Later that night, I reflected on the events of the day and the role I played in them, wondering if I could have done things differently. *Should I have taken Craig's threats more seriously? Should I have been tougher or more aggressive when he tried to get in the first time?* Hindsight is a wonderful thing and I would probably have done all those things, but I didn't know who I was dealing with. We often don't.

I take consolation from the fact that while it was hard enough not letting him in, imagine how hard it would have been to get him out! And imagine how much carnage he could have caused on the way through? We've seen mass shootings in public places like this happen in America. It could easily have happened here. I'm just very, very glad I didn't let him in.

I have security guards to help me keep out the undesirables. Who's going to help you keep out your undesirables? Think carefully about who you let into your business because once they're in, they'll be very, very difficult to get out.

'Don't let them in' extends to corporate customers too

If you're just starting out, or you've just bought a business, chances are money is tight. You're probably doing everything yourself as well. As a result, you don't have time to vet everything that comes your way, including customers. This may sound counterintuitive, but 'don't let them in' can also apply to customers. One bad customer — a customer who either takes up so much of your time you can't focus on what needs to be done, or a customer who doesn't pay on time—can bring you down. But this kind of risk can be avoided if you ask the right questions before you strike up a deal.

HOW TO GO BROKE BEFORE YOU'VE EVEN BEGUN

Claire had a software product that was quite experimental but of great interest to the energy sector. A big power company expressed interest in taking it on. Claire was delirious with excitement. One big customer like this could set her up for years. They may be the only client she ever needs.

They offered her a contract, a lucrative one, she signed it and started work. Happy days. The only trouble was, the big power company took six months to pay her invoice. Officially, they said it would take three months, but what with all the initial meetings, procurement and onboarding, the time frame blew out to six. Claire, meanwhile, not knowing about these harsh terms of payment, hired a team of software developers, data scientists and a raft of other highly paid consultants to deliver on the project. She'd paid them out of her own funds, but she was relying on the invoice being paid to help her keep it going. She asked for the payment to be fast tracked but the procurement time frames had been set and the company wasn't prepared to amend them. The upshot? Claire couldn't make wages. The team found work elsewhere, and the contract was cancelled because she couldn't deliver on the milestones. It was a disaster. Claire had lost her client, and her business, before she'd even got started.

It wasn't Claire's fault that the company took so long to pay, but if she'd known in advance that they'd take this long, she could have organised supply chain finance or something similar to tide her over, chosen to forego the contract or asked her team to work for equity.

It takes guts to ask the difficult questions—like 'How long will it take you to pay me?' or 'Can we fast track this payment as we need it for cash flow?'—especially when you're desperate for customers, and you want to present yourself in a professional manner. But if you don't, you run the risk of losing the business anyway, so you may as well speak up, set the rules or at least ask for help.

Don't just know the rules, set the rules

'Don't let them in' is not just a policy for customers and employees. It extends to investors too. I've had a few corporate Craigs try to get in and take over my business and various boards I've been on. They're exactly the same as the double-denim Craig (just better dressed). While Craig used physical coercion to get his way, the corporate Craigs use financial and legal coercion to get theirs, and will stop at nothing to win. People like this, often sociopathic and narcissistic or a delightful blend of both, can be as dangerous to you and your business as Craig was to me and mine. They are smart, calculating, often cashed up and use the courts as their personal playground for sorting out disputes.

I understand why so many business owners often get taken down by people like this. They're desperate for investors, eager to be agreeable and don't do the due diligence needed to assess if these people, and their money, are the right fit for their business.

So, how do you keep investors like these out when you've worked so bloody hard to get them in, especially if you don't know them well to start with? It all begins and ends with a simple little document called the constitution. Well, it's not that simple and it's not that little, but I didn't want to deter you from reading on because your constitution could save you from having your company stolen away from you.

When you bring investors on board, the constitution is without a doubt one of *the* most important documents you will ever issue. Why? Because it's the guidelines for how you'll engage with your investors: resolve disputes, make decisions, spend money, report back and more. The trick is to ensure that *you* set the rules of the constitution so that you control the game from the start.

Don't wait until you're successful to create and establish the 'rules'. Work them out now and get professional help to create these guidelines because one investor brought in on the wrong terms can bring you down before you've even begun. If your end game is to sell the business, then put the constitution in place early on so that you have a business to sell.

In other words, if you know the rules, you can reap many rewards, including a world championship medal, and I mean that literally.

KNOW THE RULES BEFORE YOU PLAY THE GAME

Tim Ferriss, the famous author and productivity guru, is renowned for creating hacks that get him quick results. In his first book, *The 4-Hour Work Week,* he tells of his overriding passion to win a world championship gold medal in a sport. He didn't care how or what he won the gold medal for; he just wanted to win one so he could own the bragging rights. He did his homework and landed on a sport that was steeped in tradition and therefore wide open to being hacked by someone who had scant regard for things like that. The sport? Kickboxing.

Here's how he did it.

He thoroughly researched the rules of the sport and discovered an arcane technicality that stated if a contestant stepped outside the fighting circle three times, they would be disqualified. Armed with this knowledge and an overpowering urge to win, he manoeuvred his body to force his opponents to do just that, winning a world championship and going down in the annals of history for that sport.

Was the win legal? Yes.

Honourable? Not so much.

Will most people forget how he won it? Probably.

Let me be clear. I am a big fan of Tim Ferriss, though I don't necessarily endorse his 'winning at all costs' approach. But what I do endorse is his dedication to researching the rules of his chosen sport to see how he could use those rules to his advantage. We all have access to the rules of our chosen game. Whether it's corporation law, tax law or gambling law, it's our duty to study the laws, know them and work within them as best we can to our advantage.

Tim's story illustrates three lessons:

1. You can achieve anything if you set your mind to it.

2. You can use the rules to your favour.

3. Those who don't know all the rules—or choose not to play by them—will be beaten by those who do, irrespective of time, talent and training.

Increasingly, the people who rise to the top and have an advantage (in all walks of life) are no longer those who accomplish truly great things, but those who figure out how to make the rules work for them.

So, what are the rules of how your business operates? They are yours to define, but once you do, they are placed in the constitution and everyone, including you and your investors, is duty bound and legally obligated to follow them. It goes without saying that if you don't craft your constitution carefully, you can lose big time and not even know about it until it's too late.

The reason I know so much about constitutions is because when I set up my first constitution, I got it terribly wrong and nearly lost control of my business. Here's what happened.

How a faulty constitution nearly cost me my business

When I set up my first investment fund to buy a bigger pub and attract investors, my lawyer inadvertently created a constitution that didn't work for the benefit of the fund, nor that of the business. It was a simple mistake and it came down to numbers. My constitution said 100 per cent of our shareholders had to vote on and approve financial decisions. This one clause really tripped us up as it now meant, moving forward, that if we wanted to do anything, from something as simple as buying paint or a new pool table, right through to major decisions like refinancing or renovating the building, we had to get 100 per cent of the shareholders to agree and approve it, every single time.

Can you imagine how limiting this would have been to us? We'd need to call a meeting to approve the purchase of a pot plant!

My saving grace was I knew all the investors personally and they were all great people who understood how limiting this clause was. I asked them if they would approve an amendment to the constitution, which would state that we would need only 65 per cent of the shareholders to approve decisions. Fortunately, they agreed and it gave us a great deal more freedom to be more agile and pivot quickly when lucrative opportunities arose.

(We landed upon 65 per cent as a figure, but depending on your company structure, or your personal need for control, you may want to ensure you only need the approval of 51 per cent of the shareholders.)

Ultimately, you want to retain as much control over your company as you can while ensuring the shareholders still have a say in the important decisions.

Not everyone has your best interests at heart

When it comes time to create your constitution, turn to the experts—your accountant and lawyer—and don't move a muscle until you do. Don't think you can do this on your own; you almost certainly can't, especially if you don't have a financial or legal background. You're dealing with people's money, money they've worked bloody hard to obtain, and you need to protect yourself, but you also need to protect them from other investors who may not be as aligned with your vision as you want.

You can't assume that everyone has the same goals or vision as you. For example, some investors may want to take dividends when you'd rather invest them back into the business. Some investors may not want to invest in capital improvements because this will tie up funds that could have been considered profit. Some may have a short-term view of their investment, whereas you are prepared to forgo profits for a long-term win.

There are lots of reasons why you can have misaligned investors on board, and some of those investors won't reveal their true motivations until they are already on board (or worse, on the Board).

SILENT BUT DEADLY

A colleague of mine, Patrick, had an investor in his business who was happy to be a silent partner: an investor who would sit back, not attend meetings and just pick up the dividends. But when Patrick wanted to sell his share of the business, the silent partner suddenly got very loud, and while the silent partner couldn't block the sale of the shares, he certainly could (and did) hold up the sale with a slew of lawsuits designed to delay, defer and deny Patrick the right to sell his tranche of shares.

The result?

Patrick was denied access to the proceeds of the sale of his own business for two years. Patrick was also under a non-compete restraint so he couldn't work in the same sector, which meant he effectively had no income for two years. Fortunately, he was down to his last $20 million and was able to live off the proceeds of that, but for those who can't exist without income for that long, it could have been disastrous.

Choose your investors carefully

There are ways to avoid these kinds of things happening. For a start, try not to let people who don't have your best interests (or that of the business) into the room in the first place. Second, you must select your investors with as much caution as you do your staff. They are all part of your team—and make no mistake, a bad investor can stuff you up just as easily as an errant employee. Don't think minor investors with tiny shares can't stuff you up as well. If they all band together they can have significant sway too and take the business down a road you don't want to go.

Trust, but check

When you're starting out, and you're getting traction from interested investors, it's natural to want to act fast, secure their interest and get the money in. It's also tempting to take shortcuts and use low-cost corporate documentation and legal templates sourced from a well-meaning buddy, a kind uncle or the internet. The only trouble is, when you get them checked out by a reputable lawyer, they won't accept those templates as they'll want to use their own documents (so they can charge you more!). They'll also want to take responsibility for giving you accurate documentation so that they can defend it, and you, if push comes to shove. You may as well just hire a respected lawyer to get it done right in the first place.

When you do get the official documents back from lawyers and accountants, and you're ready to send it all off to the investors for signing, read through every line very carefully, ask questions, think of the worst-case scenario, ensure you understand every sentence—every clause—and then go through it all again.

If possible, try to engage an industry-specific lawyer who knows your industry well. It will be a premium worth paying. You can find one by getting in touch with your industry association.

HOW ONE ROGUE CLAUSE COST SUSANNAH $100 000

Susannah, a fashion designer, and her business partner Abdullah, won a place on a prestigious accelerator for start-ups in the fashion sector. It was a hotly contested program and they were stoked to be chosen, especially as they were given $100 000 seed capital in exchange for 12 per cent of their company. They were so thrilled they didn't bother to read the shareholder agreement put before them by the accelerator, assuming that this reputable organisation would not ask them to sign something that was unfair or unreasonable. After all, they were 'partners', now, weren't they?

Fast forward six months, and the business has not gone well. The business partners have fallen out, the software doesn't work, they've got no customers and they've spent the seed funding on an expensive website, wages and software development and have zero runway left. But worse is yet to come. The accelerator, activating a tiny but important clause in the shareholder agreement (which Susannah and her business partner failed to notice), now want their $100 000 investment back as the duo has failed to deliver on the stated outcomes.

Not only is the business kaput but they've had to take a loan out to pay back the accelerator, leaving them in debt and despair. If they'd read the paperwork before signing, they may have done things differently, or at least been aware of their obligations before blowing all the funds.

Susannah and Abdullah were tripped up because there was a clause in the paperwork that they either didn't know was there, or did know but didn't understand. They trusted the accelerator but didn't take the time to ask questions or get advice from an expert. The duo's visionary zeal and preference to look at the bigger picture meant they missed important details, which cost them $100 000.

So, here's a tip: Don't *ever* read or sign important documents when you're hungry or tired. It's the worst mistake you can make. While it's tempting to think you can 'whip through it', you'll miss important distinctions because your energy is low. Resolve to get a good feed or a good sleep and attack it first thing the next day.

This sounds pretty obvious, right? But you'd be amazed at how often people sign documents that commit them to a range of responsibilities without even reading the document. Maybe taking care of details like this is not your 'thing'. Unfortunately, it has to become your 'thing' or it will cost you, like it did Susannah and Abdullah.

What's your blind spot?

My daughter is learning to drive right now and I'm constantly reminding her to 'check her blind spot' so that she can see any danger coming from behind. The mirrors can catch most things coming, but not everything, so she has to physically turn her head to see if there's a motorbike or a car sitting in that hard-to-see space.

Most of us have psychological blind spots too: a persistent lack of insight or awareness about a specific area of our behaviour or personality. Why do we have it? Mainly because recognition of our true feelings and motives would be painful, but more simply put, because we 'don't know what we don't know' or even simpler, we don't do things we are not good at, don't like or don't enjoy. Blind spots have cost more than one smart business owner their livelihood. It cost Susannah hers. We all have them, so if you can spot yours before it trips you up, you'll be ahead of the game.

Sometimes we're definitely aware of our blind spots, which is a good thing. Then it's no longer a blind spot, which is also a good thing because we can deal with it. But if we don't want to deal with it, or change our behaviour to address it, we turn it into our 'identity' and that absolves us of the need to deal with it because it's 'just who we are'. How convenient.

These (limiting) identities show up in all sorts of ways in the workplace, and are normally prefaced with people saying, 'I'm not good with...' It could be:

'I'm not good with numbers.'

'I'm not good with people.'

'I'm not good with detail.'

We can't all be good at everything. Your blind spot could be networking, finance, following up or customer care. Find it, acknowledge it and hire someone who can help you do it before it causes you trouble. My blind spot was marketing.

MY OWN LIMITING BELIEF

My limiting identity was 'I'm not good with marketing', which was a problem since pubs live and die on marketing. Our trivia nights, meal specials, bottle shops and sports bars all need to be marketed on Facebook, Instagram and other platforms, and if that doesn't get done, we lose big time. When I looked a bit deeper, I realised that my belief about myself was simply based on the fact that I didn't like marketing, I wasn't trained in marketing and I preferred to invest my time in activities that I enjoyed and came easy to me, which were numbers and finance.

Once I recognised that my limiting belief about my marketing ability was costing me sales, profits, growth and all the things that good marketing brings, I decided to bring someone on board who was good at marketing.

When I found the right marketing person for me, I got creative about how to pay her so that it worked for both of us. I wanted to bring her on board as a trusted partner, not just as an employee. Here's how I did it.

In short, I created a contract that gave her a share of the business. This served three purposes: it reduced my risk, reduced my payroll and incentivised her to work harder than she would if she was just a staff member. We've never looked back. I'll share more of how that contract was constructed a bit later, but sharing the spoils of war is a terrific way to get good people working for you without incurring massive staff wages.

(I appreciate that not everybody can afford to bring a staff member on or hire a consultant to do the work we're not cut out to do, but you can find great support on all the freelancer platforms for a fraction of what it used to cost.)

How to find your blind spot

If you're not aware of your own blind spots, or limiting beliefs (or identities), they can be very costly and can create all manner of headaches down the track. For example, I often see employees sign their employment contract without even reading the contract. I say, 'Do you think you'd better read that before you sign it?' and they say, 'Nah, we trust you'. I advise them to read it again and make sure they fully understand, before they sign it.

When I ask them why they haven't read it, they say, 'I didn't have time', 'I'm not smart enough to understand it' or 'I'm not good with detail'. That may be true, but it doesn't absolve them from not knowing what they're doing. Those limiting beliefs (and they're nothing but limiting beliefs) will trip you up, and will continue to trip you up until the pain they create outweighs the effort it takes to deal with them.

For the most part, you may never have to refer to the contract again, but when conflict arises, people will rush to review the contract and discover to their dismay that they agreed to something they never intended. It's too late to do much about it then. It could be decades later that this debacle comes back to haunt you. Whatever you do, don't sign something you don't understand. Don't assume the lawyers will pick everything up. They won't. And they won't take responsibility for it when they don't either. You can't say, 'Hey lawyer, you said "sign this document"—I did and now the shit has hit the fan. It's your fault, and I want my money back'.

They'll just say, 'Caveat emptor, my friend. Caveat emptor (buyer beware). And here's my invoice for telling you that, in six-minute increments'.

What you sign now has the potential to come back and haunt you many years later. You'll probably even have forgotten what you signed, but I can assure you, their lawyers won't. Because when the shit hits the fan—and if you're doing anything remotely risky, interesting or worthwhile, then it will—the first thing their lawyer will ask to look at is the constitution. And from there, all things hence will flow.

Do your homework. Do your due diligence. Check your blind spots. Identify your limiting beliefs. Acknowledge what you're not good at, and either take the time to get good at it, or delegate it to someone who is. The consequences of not doing that can be catastrophic.

FINDING YOUR BLIND SPOT

Socrates was right. 'Know thyself.' We need to know our blind spots and our limiting beliefs. They're easy to identify. Just complete the following: 'I'm not good at ...' and you'll discover them pretty quickly.

If you can't think of anything, ask your staff to complete the question for you, about you. They'll certainly have a few suggestions for you. By the way, it pays to get your staff to complete the question for themselves too. If they don't trust the process (or you) they'll probably fudge the truth and give you a furphy answer.

If that's the case, ask them to complete a profiling tool like Myers–Briggs Type Indicator (MBTI), or for a quicker, lighter version of that, try DiSC. These tools are weighted to ensure that participants don't game the outcome. In a glance, you can see what your team's strengths are and you can place everyone in a role that suits them. Lots of people who haven't had the benefit of profiling dismiss it, saying, 'You can't put people in boxes' or 'No two people are alike', but I disagree.

Taking the time to learn how your team works, what they value and how to motivate them is the best investment you can make in yourself, in them and in your business.

Act in haste, repent at leisure

I have an affinity for numbers and detail so I'm always going to be drilling down into documents to see what's working and what's not. I take the time to do it because I'm good at it and I enjoy it. But if you're not like me, then you'll either need to 'take the time' to learn it, start 'thinking like a lawyer/accountant' and do the legwork to understand it, or you could find yourself on the wrong end of a contract and losing control of the decision making, how you spend your money and ultimately, losing control of the company.

How can we overcome these limiting beliefs?

It all comes down to mindset and time.

Find the time to learn

When I was around 19 years old, I was walking home from work, and I saw an elderly gentleman in his front yard. He was probably about 40 but to my young eye he looked positively geriatric. He was on his front lawn repairing a carburettor from the EJ Holden that sat in his driveway. He had all the parts splayed out on the lawn and was methodically tending to each piece, inspecting each in detail to see what was malfunctioning.

I stopped and watched him, intrigued with the patience and persistence he displayed in detecting the rogue element.

I said, 'I wish I could repair stuff like that but I'm no good with cars'. He said, 'You could fix it if you took the time to learn it'.

Wham! That comment hit me like a tonne of bricks. He didn't mean to sound rude; he was just stating a fact, but I was taken aback with the gravitas of what he said.

He was right. I could almost certainly fix that simple piece of machinery if I took the time to learn; if I took the time to pull it apart, see how it all fitted together and saw what made it tick. In fact, I could probably turn my hand to most things if I took the time to learn them. As could you; as could anyone. The question is: Do we take the time? For most of us, the answer is no. But imagine if we did? Imagine how many problems we could avoid in our lives if we just 'took the time' to work them out.

HOW NOT 'FINDING THE TIME' COST MICK HIS BUSINESS

Mick and I went to school together. He became a carpenter; I went into pubs. He runs his own small business so he used to pop into my pub after work on a Friday for a beer and tell me how things were going. His SUV truck was his 'office' and all his tools of the trade were in the back of it. He had a limiting belief that he was 'not good with detail'. In fact, he was excellent at detail, when it suited him. If he was trimming a piece of timber he'd spend an hour just getting the measurements right. But when it came to lodging business paperwork and getting his financial documents in order, his limiting belief kicked in. In reality, he was good with detail, but he chose not to 'take the time' to deal with an area of his business that he didn't enjoy.

It all started when he moved house. He subsequently forgot to let the insurance company know about his change of address. As a result, he didn't receive the policy renewal paperwork in the mail, which meant he didn't sign the policy renewal, which meant he didn't pay the policy, which meant he wasn't insured.

So, when his truck got stolen and all his tools along with it (literally the 'tools of his trade'), he was not only not covered for the theft of the tools, he was also not covered for the theft of his vehicle, all of which he had to go out and replace, at his own cost. Had he just sent the email to the insurance company about the change of address, he would have been covered for everything, including loss of income (as there was a clause in there that covered him for that too). The cost? Fifty thousand dollars in tools, $70 000 for the truck and $100 000 in lost work that he had to forgo because he couldn't complete the existing work or start the new jobs he had lined up.

Now he's in debt to pay for the tools (he took out a loan to buy them), the car (he took out a loan for that too) and he had to pay back the customers the deposits he had taken for work he could no longer complete. The upshot? He closed down the business and went to work for a construction company. Now he's still in debt, and worse, an employee, working for 'the man' and hating every minute of it. All because, in his words, 'he's not good with detail'. It could all have been avoided if he'd made one phone call or sent one email to the insurance company. That's a costly own goal.

Was Mick good at detail? Not really, but he also *chose* not to be. That was his identity. In reality, he just didn't take the time to do what he needed to do, which was inform the insurance company of his change of address. That one, simple action would have saved him from losing everything. Most of us are not good at something; we all have that blind spot. *Find* that something, because it could be the thing that causes your downfall.

THE '3 LANGUAGES OF STEVE': WHY WE ALL NEED TO BE MULTILINGUAL

Doing what I love—serving beers, chatting with customers.

I am a pretty easy-going guy and I pride myself on being able to connect with people from all walks of life. This quality has come in handy because my business demands I play multiple roles. Depending on what day it is, or what meeting I am in, I will be called on to speak many different languages and project multiple identities.

For example, when I'm in the front bar of my pub, I need to be 'publican Steve': the cheery, friendly guy who owns the pub; the guy who shakes everyone's hand, welcomes them in, pours them a beer and has a yarn.

When I'm at an investor update meeting, I need to be 'financial' Steve: the private equity fund manager who is across all the details—the numbers, the percentages, the ratios and the rates of return. They have questions, and my team and I need to give them answers.

When I'm reviewing contracts for sale, or supplier agreements, or employment memos, I need to be 'lawyer Steve': the legal guy who picks up the inconsistencies in clauses or definitions; the guy who challenges the lawyers to justify their case and has the blue pen in hand underlining subsection 4, part 8, clause 5 because it contains variations that weren't in the original contract.

Depending on what industry you're in, you'll need to play multiple roles and speak multiple 'languages' too.

Play and learn

One of my favourite philosophies is 'play and learn'. It may sound like a segment from the TV show *Play School* (and it could be) but I can assure you it's a very adult principle, and one that I have employed many times over with great effect.

For example, when I use technology—and I'm the first to admit while I'm not a philistine or a technophobe, I sometimes need to call on my teenage kids to help me change a setting or download an app. But I digress. When I use technology, and this is a metaphor for other areas in life, if I am so scared of pushing a button that I don't touch any button, how will I learn? Sure, I may delete a database or two or send a random file to the wrong person, but at least I've learned what not to do next time.

This fear of getting it wrong stops us from doing many of the things we need, and ought, to do. If I'm too scared of changing the pub menu, how will I know what my patrons like? If I'm too scared of asking for investors to trust me with their hard-earned money, how will I know what pitch works and what doesn't? How will I grow the business if I'm not prepared to make a mistake?

USE TIME WISELY

People often say, 'Steve, you have five children, 350 staff, seven pubs and over $100 million in assets under management. How do you find the time to do it all?' The answer is I am ruthlessly efficient with my use of time. I use it wisely and find any opportunity to multitask so I can get more done.

For example, I live on a four-acre property in regional New South Wales and had to commute to Sydney by train for a few months to complete a project. I could have listened to music or read a novel, but I detest wastage of any sort, especially time, so I used the time to study for my MBA. The train was like a library, but better. It was quiet, had good Wi-Fi, comfy seats, a nice view, and best of all, no interruptions. The coffee was shite but hey, you can't have it all.

We all get given the same amount of time per day. The difference is in how you use it.

Keep learning

Benjamin Franklin said, 'An investment in education pays the highest return' and I totally agree. I did much of my hospitality training at TAFE and have nothing but praise for the institution. I learned some very practical skills that have served me well ever since. I helped them develop the accreditation that trains up our new crop of industry leaders, and genuinely love giving back to the institution that gave me so much. I was just a young adult when I studied at TAFE and I did wonder if the time and effort would be worth it, but my philosophy centred on these key questions: 'Where will this course take me? Is it part of a bigger picture? If this is a diploma, will it count towards a degree? Will the degree get me to my Master's? Can I build upon this?' I like to feel that whatever I'm doing is playing a part in getting me to the next stage.

Summing up...

1. It's easier to keep people out of your business than to get rid of them once they're in.

2. Choose your customers as carefully as you choose your staff and investors. Know the rules before you play the game, or they will get made for you.

3. What you sign today will come back to haunt you when you least expect it.

4. Don't assume everyone on your team wants what you want.

5. Choose your investors carefully.

6. Find the time to learn what you need to learn, even if you don't like doing it.

7. Give yourself a break if you make a mistake. We're all human.

CHAPTER 3
Find your values

It is not living that matters, but living rightly.

Socrates

I live life by the rules of karma (most of the time anyway). It helps me see the best in people and provides a nice reason for having hope when things don't go so well. My definition of karma is doing the right thing, no matter what.

Do the right thing

They say a good liar needs a good memory to keep track of all the lies they tell. Why not just tell the truth? That way you don't need to remember a thing, and it frees up your brain to focus on more productive endeavours. Then you can move forward with vigour and not be looking in the rearview mirror all the time, hoping and praying that someone, somewhere, doesn't catch up with you.

Doing the right thing all the time is not for the faint hearted. It can be tiring, inconvenient, expensive and there's certainly no guarantee that your efforts or actions will be rewarded. But just because you don't get an immediate reward doesn't mean you shouldn't do it; knowing you made a difference to someone else's life is reward enough. Yeah, I know I sound like Mother Teresa, but I've had enough experiences with karma to know that if you do the right thing, you'll be rewarded for it — if not materially, at least emotionally. (Although I do smile a little when karma pays a visit to someone who deserves it.) But all jokes aside, the reward is knowing that you can lay your head on your pillow at night without fearing what the next phone call or email may deliver, knowing you did the right thing and that you (possibly) made a difference to someone else's life.

Karma comes back

I've had first-hand experience with karma. It was in 1997 and I was running my first pub, The Thurles Castle in Sydney. It was a tough gig, especially for a first-time pub licensee, as the pub was located in Chippendale, a rough inner-city suburb, smack bang (forgive the pun) in the middle of a heroin hot spot and home to a haven of homeless souls who had fallen on hard times. Unsurprisingly, it was well known for having the highest rate of crime in the country. So, to say that something interesting was always happening there was an understatement. For a first-time licensee like me, it was a baptism by fire.

Despite all that, or maybe because of it, the area had a terrific sense of community so when something bad happened, my locals told me who the culprits were and we could sort it out without getting the authorities involved every time.

The environment wasn't all bad. I met my wife while I was working there and have since had five children with her, so some good has come of it. I guess. Just kidding! And the friendships that were forged in those early years are still as strong today as they were then. Those days were never, ever dull.

But there was one incident that sticks with me which reinforced that doing the right thing is the right thing to do, even if it's uncomfortable, impractical or financially deleterious to do so.

It was around midnight on a wet and cold Saturday night. One of my lovely locals, an older lady called Cath, was leaving the pub. Just as she was pulling out of the car park, a man in a balaclava took out a hammer and bashed through her window, leaned in, pulled out the keys from the ignition, reached across and grabbed her handbag from the passenger seat.

We heard this almighty scream outside and raced out to the car park. When we got to Cath's car, I saw this figure in black flee across the intersection and onto the other side of the street. I didn't think twice. I raced after him, dodging in and out of traffic, trying to pin him down, weaving my way in between hordes of bumper-to-bumper cars. He ran down an alley between two buildings. I chased after him, not even cognisant of where I was going or how far I had run. I stopped running to get my bearings and took a look around me. I was surrounded by derelict houses, warehouses with the windows shot out and burned-out cars hoisted on bricks. It was not a nice neighbourhood. I poked around some of the empty warehouses to see if I could find him, but he was gone.

After I got my breath back, I realised, as they say, I was not in Kansas anymore. What's more, I was without my wallet and phone, and I started to feel decidedly unsafe. I hightailed it out of there and got back to the bar before this violent criminal decided to take that hammer of his and have a go at me as well to punish me for making him run.

When I got back to the bar, Cath was inside being looked after by my trusty staff. She was still shaking and had a nasty gash on her cheek from where the shattered glass had cut her. I went out to the car park, found her keys lying in the bushes and moved the car into the pub garage to keep it safe over the weekend until Cath was in a fit state to drive.

On Monday, Cath arrived at the pub to take her car to the crash repairers. She was still distraught from the events of Saturday night, red eyed from crying and in pain from the cut cheek.

'Cath, what's wrong? Your car is here, it's going to be all right,' I said.

'I know Steve but...'

'What is it Cath?'

She could barely speak for the tears coursing down her cheeks.

'Steve, I don't have insurance. I don't have any savings. I can't afford to get my car fixed. It's going to cost me a fortune. How am I going to get to work?' And the tears started to flow again.

My heart went out to her. She was a pensioner on limited income and every penny she made was hard fought for. She wasn't my mum, or my relative, but she was my customer and she'd become a mate too, so I said, 'Cath, don't worry about it. I'll take care of it. Leave it with me'.

She resisted but I insisted, and she eventually relented.

'Fix me up when you're flush,' I said, knowing that would be next to never. But I didn't care. I wanted to look after her. If it was my mum, I hoped that someone would do the same and respond in a similar fashion.

What goes around comes around

Seven months later, St Patrick's Day was upon us. Our Chippendale community was overwhelmingly Irish, so we wanted to use the day to honour them, thank them and provide them with a memory of what it would be like if they were back in the Old Country and give them a great day.

We opened at 7 am, put on a cracking breakfast of stew, soda bread and black pudding, and hired a stack of Irish bands to play out the front of the pub, in the beer garden and down a side street. We decorated the pub in every shade of green you can imagine, and flew the Irish flag high. It was all happening. Even Brendan Gleeson, the wonderful Irish actor from the *Harry Potter* film came in to see what all the fuss was about.

A few kilometres down the road at a local park, a massive Irish festival was underway. It was an official event sponsored by the Irish Consulate and *The Irish Echo*, a magazine for the expatriate community. Unlucky for them, it started to rain, and with our bar just around the corner, the festival patrons took shelter in our pub. We had four bar staff (including Kris, a trusted staff member who started with me back then and is still with me today—and is also godfather to my son Rory), which was the most we ever needed, even on our busiest nights as it was quite a small pub and we only had one bar area that served the entire pub.

As the rain came down, the crowd came in. To put it mildly, we were getting smashed. There were queues out the door. People were lining up five deep trying to get a drink. The patrons weren't angry—they could see we were working as fast as we could go—but it was painful not having the space or staff available to sell as many drinks as we could have.

It wasn't just the bar staff getting smashed either. The empties on tables were stacking up, the dishwasher was running at full tilt and the kegs were being tapped as quickly as we could muster. I rallied around to get more staff to come in but at such short notice, no-one was available. It got so busy my bar staff would pour three beers at once, put them in front of the locals who were lining up, and say 'pay me later' so that they could move on to the next customer. And you know what? Every single one of them came in the next day and paid their tab. To the cent. How's that for honesty?

It gets better.

One of the locals said to his mate, 'Steve needs a hand,' and without asking for thanks or permission, he stood up, walked over to the tables and started stacking the empty glasses and taking them to the kitchen. The stack got so high, it nearly hit the 13-foot ceiling. That's how many glasses they were collecting. And despite him not being a trained bar professional, he did not drop a glass.

His mate then got up off the stool, walked behind the bar and started pouring beers for the customers. Two others headed down to the cellar to grab more glasses and brought them up and proceeded to stack the glass tray so the bartenders had a fresh supply of glasses coming through.

These three guys, Donal, Chris and Nick, didn't just help out for a minute or two: they worked 10 hours straight, without taking a break, and without asking for money. With their help, and just four bar staff, we served over 11 000 drinks that day. In today's terms, that's the equivalent of taking $80 000 in one day, which for a tiny pub on a suburban street is a great achievement, and one I couldn't even contemplate achieving without the help of my loyal community. (Incidentally, those three men became lifelong buddies and have all gone on to have highly successful business careers. It's not surprising. The values they showed that day are the values that will take anyone to the top of their chosen field.)

It touched me greatly to see my locals—people I knew, but didn't really know well—stand up, pitch in and help in such a generous and selfless way. They worked their arses off, for no pay, just because they wanted to help me in my hour of need.

I learned a valuable lesson that day. Community is everything. I knew that to be true anyway, but I had never seen it in action the way I did that day. I also learned that community is a two-way street. When I think back to how we helped Cath that night when she was in her hour of need, we too were helped by people who owed us nothing in our hour of need. What goes around comes around.

Want free marketing? Find your community

Facebook is everything in our business. Instagram's important too, but Facebook is the king when it comes to quickly getting the word out about something. During COVID-19, we often put out posts promoting half-priced take-away meals. We knew that our community were doing it tough in lockdown (both psychologically and financially), so we wanted to do something to help them. Within minutes of the post going up, we had 100 orders.

But there's something that's equally important, much cheaper (free actually) and exponentially more powerful than social media marketing—and that's *community marketing*. In other words, do the right thing by your community, look after them, treat them well (before you need to and without any expectation of that goodwill being returned) and you may discover that your community do your social media marketing for you as well.

The world's obsession with social media has obscured how important it is to connect in person with the people in your community. Your local community is a rich, untapped vein of new business, yet is often overlooked in favour of advertising on social media, radio or elsewhere. Irrespective of what business you have, or what you sell, it pays to place yourself and your business at the heart of your community. What does this even mean? For a start, look at where you're located.

As a starting point, jump onto Google Maps, and draw a circle around the map with a radius of 3 kilometres with your business in the centre. Then analyse all the businesses within that 3-kilometre radius. Who's there? Who can you help? How can you serve them? What collaborations can you create with them?

Do the same with the people who reside within that area. Go to the Australian Bureau of Statistics website, or your local council website, and review the demographics of the residential area. Are they young families? Singles? Well-off professionals? Senior citizens? Middle-aged mums? Whatever it is, brainstorm what your business has in common with them, work out what they need that you could offer and create a win–win for you both.

HOW TO GET FREE MARKETING

If you play your cards right and don't mind doing a little bit of 'guerrilla' marketing, you can get big returns for a small investment. For example, when we renovated The Kent pub in Hamilton, New South Wales, we did our due diligence (as always) and discovered that a major bank was building their offices around the corner, that the nearby sports stadium was home to over a dozen sporting codes and that a new housing development targeting young families was going up around the corner. Once we knew that, we used that information to put ourselves at the heart of the community. We did simple things that we knew they'd like and appreciate. For example, we:

- dropped lunch menus at the reception desk of the commercial buildings in the area

- gave them all a loyalty card so they got a free coffee when they bought their first lunch from us

(continued)

- sponsored the local sporting club and invited them to have their after-game celebrations and award nights at our pub so that they had a communal place to celebrate (or commiserate)

- employed the local footy and netball players as wait staff at our pubs

- joined the local Chamber of Commerce and got to know the members, contributed to the workings of the clubs and offered valuable support

- donated food and drinks to the Rotary groups when they ran a sausage sizzle at Bunnings or hosted the local art show.

It's activities like these that put the 'social' into social media and make marketing a much easier, and cheaper, endeavour than it might otherwise be.

We don't do it just to get a business result (but that's definitely a nice side effect of being a community-focused business), we do it because for many regional communities, a pub is the centre of the town, the village and the community, and the hub around which all things circulate.

Match your purpose to the concept

When creating the 'concept' for your business, it needs to be a combination of what you can provide for the local community and what your strengths are. If there's no overlap, then find the right people who can help you plug the gaps. For example, when it comes to hiring staff, even if you don't personally love sport but your business is surrounded by sports stadiums, hire staff who live and breathe sport so they can pick up the slack for whatever you can't, or don't, want to get involved with.

Obviously, I can't be at the coal face of every pub every day, so I hire the local footy and netball players as our wait staff. Not only am I giving the local kids a job, who do you think is going to come in and visit those kids when they're working? Their friends, and lots of them. Not only do they all drink, eat and party up a storm, but when we need new staff, who do you think does our recruitment? Our staff. We pay them a recruitment fee if the person works out and everyone wins.

Another side benefit of hiring the locals is that if one or another of them can't make a shift, they do a ring-around and find one of their mates to do it for them, taking that headache off our plates for us. And the community reciprocation cycle just keeps giving back. Where do you think those bar staff are going to come when they have a night off? To the pub where they work because their friends are working that night.

We also make a point of hiring local bands to play at our pubs. We do it for the same reasons, but also because we love to think that we're giving a local kid a shot and we love the thought that when they become a big name we can say, 'They got their start at the Sea Breeze Hotel', or wherever they were playing. We love helping our community like this and we certainly gain more back than we could ever give.

If you treat your community right, you'll find your community will treat you right as well. What's important here is intention. Of course, we have our marketing hats on when we do this, hoping to see a commercial return. But we do it anyway because it's the right thing to do. If you're part of a community, and you want it to support you, you need to give back to it and place yourself at the centre of your community.

MARKETING TO MIDDLE-AGED AND RETIRED MEN

One of our pubs, The Ocean View, is in Urunga, a picturesque seaside town around 500 kilometres north of Sydney. The town has a Men's Shed, located a kilometre from the pub. (A Men's Shed is like a 'community garage' for retired men who want to get out of the house, build connections, do something useful and give back.) The movement was established around 2007 and has become a wonderful way for men to get out from under the feet of their wives, who can't cope with them being at home after 40 years of not.

(continued)

Our local Men's Shed comprises some retired but talented and experienced carpenters, engineers and farmers, so when we need any handy work done—from building a table, to paving a courtyard or painting a wall—we ask the guys at the Men's Shed if they can do it for us. We pay them market rates, they take great pride in their workmanship and it gives them a sense of purpose and pride to know that they, and their skills, are (still) valuable.

What we quickly discovered is that our mission to place ourselves in the heart of the community and connect with local groups like this had an incredible (and lucrative) knock-on effect. For example, when we engaged the guys from the Men's Shed to build a communal dining table for us, not only did they do an incredible job, but they brought their wives, kids, grandkids, cousins, drinking mates and car club buddies to the pub to show them their handiwork! And what do all these people do when they sit down to admire their man's handiwork? They drink, eat, watch sport, place a bet, play pool and then all those people tell their friends to come down and do the same, and so the 'social network' continues.

When businesses want to use social media marketing, they sometimes forget about the 'social' bit and just focus on marketing. We don't. We know that putting ourselves at the heart of any community is not only good for business, it's good for the community.

When you do this, you'll find that the community will do the marketing for you.

Put yourself in the right room

I constantly seek to improve myself and my business, and am always alert to situations or experiences that can help me achieve that. A few years back, I was at a certain stage of my business journey when I felt I wasn't growing my network or expanding my mind. I wanted to take myself and my business to the next level, so I did what I always do when I have a knowledge gap and enrolled in a course.

The first one I took was a short course on entrepreneurship, which was so rewarding I went further and enrolled in a Masters of Business (MBA).

I enjoyed that so much I wanted to enrol in an executive course for leaders. But where? What was the best one? I did my research and decided that if I was going to be away from the family, and invest time and money on myself and my business, then I may as well aim high. And what's the best business school in the world? Harvard. That's where I was going to go. I completed the entrance and aptitude tests, provided them with a glowing reference (written by my superstar PA Wendy!), booked my tickets, said goodbye to my wife and babies and hightailed it to Harvard, Boston, the alma mater of legends like Bill Gates, Matt Damon and a host of American presidents. I couldn't have been more excited.

Trying to keep the jetlag at bay and stay awake long enough to morph into the new time zone, I hunted down *Cheers*, the bar made famous in the eponymous TV show. The locals were as friendly as they were on TV. My body clock was pegged at 3 am but it was 7 pm in Boston so I had to have a beer. Hey, when in Rome...

Deep down, I was super nervous about what lay ahead. When under pressure, my brain veers into a negative mindset and I start to doubt myself. I started thinking, 'What right do I have to be here? Who did I think I was, coming to Harvard? How did I get here? Would I be able to cut it? I was just a bar-room brawler from a tiny town in the regions of New South Wales and here I was walking the hallowed turf that John F. Kennedy walked on. I needed to get out of this unhelpful headspace, so I did what I do whenever I lack confidence or I'm nervous: I drew on all my old stories of when I'd been successful. I reread my diary notes to remind me that I had accomplished worthwhile things; I recalled positive things people had said to me over the years, like when my university lecturer in accounting, Professor Rodriguez, reviewed a paper I wrote on the financing of pubs and suggested I do a PhD on it (the fact he took me seriously and considered me capable was a huge honour in my eyes). These were just some of the techniques I used to help calm my nerves and give me the confidence to step into the classroom with some semblance of self-assurance.

On day one, they paired us up to complete a group project. I disliked my partner on first sight. Great. Out of all the people in the room I could have got paired with, I get him! He was loud, brash, cocky and thought he knew everything. He was very intimidating, wouldn't listen to anyone else and talked over everyone. In that moment, I totally regretted coming.

But as the course progressed, he chilled out a bit, I found my feet and we developed a really good relationship. Incidentally, he had every reason to be cocky. He was Lorenzo Delpani, the former CEO of Revlon Cosmetics, so he knew a thing or two about business. He played the game of business at a much higher level than me and had done deals that dwarfed mine many times over, but by virtue of us being in the same room at the same time, I gained access to his global network of business titans, a cohort of colleagues I would never have ordinarily met working in my regional town.

Some of those contacts became mentors and friends and opened a door to another world that has been instrumental in helping me access new ideas, funds and innovations. When it comes to business, it's not what you know, it's definitely who you know. Putting myself in that Harvard room paid off in ways that I could never have expected.

That experience reinforced how important it was for me and my staff to surround ourselves with people from our industry and attend as many events and conferences as possible. This helps us spot the latest trends, keep tabs on new legislation and regulation and meet potential investors, and increases our chances of being in the right room at the right time.

THINK LOCAL

I appreciate others may not be able to afford the time or money to get to Harvard, but you don't have to travel too far to find the right people and be in the right room. You can find it in your local neighbourhood. It's called the Chamber of Commerce. While it may sound like a stuffy old club for pale, stale males, it can offer many valuable opportunities. It attracts a wide range of businesspeople with diverse interests and experiences, exposes you to a range of opportunities and helps you grow your network.

I joined the Hamilton Chamber of Commerce in 2002 and in 2004 was elected the Public Officer. We often invited outside speakers to attend and deliver a presentation. One particular presenter was so outstanding I invited him to come by the pub for a beer. He swung by, I bought him a beer and we had a great chat. He said that he had always wanted to invest in a pub. Little did he know that I was right in the middle of raising capital to increase the number of pubs in my portfolio (mainly because I'm always in the middle of raising capital to increase the number of pubs in my portfolio!). I emailed him our information memorandum to buy into The Duke Hotel and The Lakeside Village Tavern and three days later he rang and said, 'We're in!' I said 'Great! But who's "we"?' and he said, 'Me, my accountant, his mate and his mate's mate!'

I couldn't help but smile. That was one of the most relaxed capital raising efforts I had ever encountered. All because I took the initiative to join my local Chamber of Commerce and buy a mate a beer.

Give to get

Attending events is critical to staying connected with your industry, but I know the concept of networking strikes fear into the hearts of most people, especially introverts. The thought of turning up to a room filled with strangers, introducing yourself to someone you've never met and trying to make small talk, can make even the most extroverted networkers quake in their boots.

But I've found over the years that if you change your focus from what you can get from the event to what you can *give*, you're more likely to make more contacts, reduce your anxiety levels and get a better result. 'Give to get' has always been a helpful motto for me. If I go in with a focus on how I can give assistance to someone, rather than get something from them, it takes the pressure off having to sell something or do anything or be someone I'm not. I can just be me; relaxed, open and ready to help.

How to network

Many people are turned off by networking because they attend the wrong events, which means they're mixing with the wrong people, which means they don't get a good outcome. You can increase your likelihood of success in connecting with the right people if you do some homework before you go. Take a moment to research the event online, check out the agenda, rehearse your pitch and link in with a few guests before you go so you have a few friendly faces to turn to when you arrive.

What not to do when networking

I recently attended a conference conducted by a family business association, and sat down to watch the opening keynote speaker. The man next to me introduced himself and I said, 'What do you do?' He said, 'I'm an accountant'. Not needing the services of an accountant, I didn't investigate much further, but had a pleasant chat all the same.

At the tea break, he handed me his card, which read, 'Accountant—Franchise Specialist'.

Well, that got my attention. We have a bar franchise called Shoeless Jack and are always on the lookout for professional services that specialise in the sector. If he'd introduced himself with, 'I'm an accountant *and I help businesses launch their franchise operation*', I would have instantly sought him out for a consultation.

Get on the stage

If you're keen to accelerate your networking efforts, don't just *attend* an event, *speak* at the event. Like most people, I'm not a natural public speaker, but I have found that one of the fastest ways to build my network, gain credibility and put myself in the right room with the right people is by being a guest speaker at an event.

If you value efficiency, being a speaker will fast track your networking efforts more than almost any other method. For example, is it more productive to schedule 10 one-hour meetings with 10 different people, or be a guest speaker in front of 100 people for one hour? You do the maths. Not only is the 'one to many' event more efficient, it's also more effective. Why? Because your credibility has already been established before you even walk on stage or utter a word, and you get one hour of uninterrupted stage time to share your words, wit and wisdom with everyone in the room. If they didn't know who you were, or what you did before the speech, they certainly will after it.

Summing up...

1. Do the right thing, always, even when it's costly, inconvenient or exhausting. Sleeping soundly at night is the reward.

2. Look after your local community and it will look after you.

3. Get out of your comfort zone and put yourself in the company of people who are achieving results that you'd like to emulate.

4. First impressions can be wrong. Don't make assumptions about people until you've spent time with them.

5. Give to get.

6. Think local before you think global.

7. Do your research before you go to a networking event so you can get the most from it.

8. If you really want to increase your network and authority, don't just attend an event. Speak at the event.

CHAPTER 4
Find your focus

... life must be understood backwards. But ... it must be lived forwards.

Søren Kierkegaard

They say that little things don't matter. Tell that to the guy with a mozzie in his tent in the middle of the outback, or the woman with a pebble in her shoe. Little things can have a big impact.

Do the little things right

I was reminded of this a while back when I was attending a seminar on applied finance in Melbourne. Across the road from my venue was a tennis centre where all the professional players in town were training for the Australian Open. Being an avid sports lover, I couldn't help but turn my attention to the courts, where Roger Federer was conducting his last-minute training for the finals that night.

I thought Roger would be practising his overhead smash shots, his service or his backhand. But no. He was on the back line, bent over, bouncing a ball, over and over.

He must have done it 50 times without a break. Occasionally, he would toss the ball up in the air, as if to serve, but then he'd just let the ball drop to the ground and go back to bouncing it, over and over. I should have been watching an accountant present on time-series analysis, but I was transfixed with watching this master of tennis rehearse his ritual, in awe at his precise preparation and attention to detail.

Knowing he had a Grand Slam tournament ahead of him that night, he could have been doing a hundred different things that afternoon to prepare for the game ahead, but he was doing the most basic thing a tennis player could do. He was bouncing the ball. When it comes to tennis, a little thing like bouncing the ball is the basic building block upon which every other move is made. Get that wrong and you're guaranteed to fail.

When it comes to running my business, I need to know what the basic building blocks of success are too; I need to know what matters. Like Roger, I have a hundred things running around in my head about what I should be focusing on. What I choose to pay attention to will determine the success or otherwise of my business because each and every day, it's the little things that get attended to that make all the difference.

Running a pub looks easy because everyone at the pub looks like they're having a good time, but I can assure you that there's a complex array of activities taking place behind the scenes to make it run smoothly. So, when I wake up in the morning and my mind inevitably turns to the events of the day, I can't help but think about the dozens, even hundreds, of things that need to be done that day. How do I know what to pay attention to? Like Roger, it comes down to knowing what matters and doing the little things right.

Success has its origin in decades past

It all starts with what you want to achieve and acknowledging each and every goal is made up of hundreds of micro activities and minor goals. If you just focus on doing the little things right, consistently, the rest will take care of itself. For example, Roger didn't just turn up on centre court as the reigning champion. He spent decades building up to it, attending kids' tennis competitions, auditioning for training academies, enjoying wins, enduring losses, suffering injuries and setbacks and more. And there he is now, decades later, slaying all before him to become arguably the world's greatest player. Every success story has its origins in decades past.

What Roger reminds me to do is just focus on the little things — the things that matter; the one percenters that underpin the entire success of the business — and to just methodically attend to them every day.

This means you need to know the minutiae of your business, the details, the little things that others might overlook. If you've ever looked at how a front bar operates you can see that there are literally hundreds of moving parts that need to be tracked, monitored, ordered, replaced, replenished. From the lemons that have to be sliced to go in the gin and tonic, to the caramel syrup that flavours a cappuccino, to the paper that goes in the EFTPOS machine. And that's just the small stuff. There are literally thousands of micro-tasks that need to be taken care of across my pub network. How do we do it? We created a robust Real Time Management Reporting (RTMR) system that tracks all our data, stock, staff, cash flow, sales and margins to help us know what's going on at any time. We rely on this to help us make fast, accurate decisions.

THE $3 MILLION GLASS OF PEPSI

Being across the detail is not just necessary, it brings in new business and is the basic building block upon which all other decisions are made. For example, I recall pitching to a sophisticated high-net-worth investor a few years ago and he asked me what it costs to serve a single glass of Pepsi. I knew the cost for a box of Pepsi syrup was $116 so I was able to calculate the answer in a heartbeat. When I asked him later why he invested he said, 'Anyone who has that level of knowledge and oversight into their business knows what they're doing'. That conversation about the $116 box of syrup landed me an investor worth over $3 million. Details matter.

I didn't just wake up and know the cost of a box of syrup. That knowledge came from working in the industry for decades, being hands on, negotiating with the suppliers, knowing the numbers, digging into the daily data. This enables me to know in an instant what is happening in that venue, in that bar, on that day.

This obsession with detail may not sound like a big deal, and could even be considered micromanaging, but it's not. We work with such slim margins that we can't afford to be cavalier with detail; it could be the difference between making a profit and a loss, between success and failure.

With over 350 staff, I obviously now delegate much of the day-to-day running of the business to them, but I can do this because I have established simple but powerful systems and structures to help me keep track of everything, so I know what's going on without having to micromanage or be there in person. Those numbers tell me everything.

A lightbulb moment

You're probably wondering, what details should you pay attention to? Only you can know what details you should pay attention to in your business, but every industry has benchmarks that reveal the 'canary in the coalmine': the things that are not going so well. (That's why you need to attend industry events—so you can find out from others what is standard and what is an anomaly.)

In my pubs, there are dozens of indicators that tell me if a pub or venue is being managed properly. For example, a mate and I had dinner at a local pub a few weeks ago. When I walked in, the first thing I noticed was one of the lightbulbs in the dining room was out. Fair enough. A bulb can blow at any time, but I noted it. I came back a week later for another meal, and the same lightbulb was still blown. That tells me things are not quite right at that venue—that they don't have any systems or procedures for dealing with maintenance. It tells me that someone, somewhere, isn't paying attention to the little things.

There are lots of visual clues in retail operations that declare little things aren't being attended to (and therefore the bigger things too); it could be the signage out the front is faded, the front door doesn't shut properly, the framed Certificate of Appreciation from the local kindergarten is dusty and dated from 2008, or the bell at the accommodation front desk doesn't work.

By extrapolation, you can be sure that this inattention to detail extends to other aspects of the business. It could be the cleanliness of the rest rooms, the handling of food, the maintenance of the ovens or fridges or the management of the finances. This inattention to minor detail can have major consequences.

We hear about fires and accidents in venues. They are terrible things to witness, but from my experience they don't just occur out of the blue. The seeds of the disaster are often sown way in advance.

ON THE SMELL OF AN OILY RAG

We had one incident in our pub that few could have predicted. One of our chefs cleaned the stove with a tea towel. Standard procedure. He put the tea towel in the washing machine and then the drier. When he did that, the residue of fat in the tea-towel fabric heated up, and continued to retain that heat long after it had been taken out of the drier. He then put it on the benchtop, and it sat there, quietly smouldering away, and then suddenly, *boom!*: it burst into flames. A spontaneous combustion of sorts. It took everybody by surprise as there had been no warning it was about to flare up. We lost a fridge and a benchtop due to the fire, but we were able to contain it to one location and extinguish it quickly before someone got hurt. We've obviously changed our cleaning policies since then to ensure this kind of random event can't happen again, but it was a warning that dangerous fires like this can be caused literally by the smell of an oily rag.

Why do I care about lightbulbs?

You might be wondering why I'm hyper-aware of busted lightbulbs. When I was 18, I worked at a local pub. I was brand new, and got given all the shit jobs to do. Fair enough. One of them was to change the busted lightbulbs. I got up on the ladder, unscrewed the bulb and got an almighty shock that ran right through my body. It paralysed me for a second. Turns out the wiring was shoddy, hadn't been maintained or inspected for years and was in danger of short circuiting the entire building. In the act of changing a single lightbulb, I could have been killed. Fast forward 30 years and I employ hundreds of young people. I don't want them being harmed or even killed because I didn't take notice of the little things.

What we pay attention to

You need to separate out what makes a difference to the business and what doesn't. To do that, you need to know your numbers. For example, 35 per cent of what we sell over the bar is draught beer, so we spend a lot of time making sure that the beer service is efficient and everything is in excellent working order.

For example, we need to make sure that the kegs are easy to access, our glasses are clean and stacked close to the tap; that the dishwasher is easy to load and fast drying so that we never run out of clean glasses; and that the till has cash and the tea towels are frequently laundered.

This may all sound bleeding obvious, but on a night when we're serving 3000 customers and pouring 30 000 beers, if those details aren't taken care of, a lot can go wrong very quickly, which means we don't serve as much beer as we should. If this happens, we lose our rebate. If that happens, we lose our margins, we become unprofitable, we lose our investors and the dominoes start to fall.

But the *fundamental building block* that underpins all this is that our beer reticulation system has to be in excellent working order and be meticulously cleaned on a regular basis. Part of the reticulation system is a $10 hose that connects the beer keg to the pouring taps and they're a bugger of a thing to keep clean, but it has to be done or the beer tastes stale and there goes 35 per cent of our alcohol sales—and that's not good for business. If that hose isn't cleaned regularly, the rest of it—the clean glasses, the stacking, the polishing, the till, the tea towels—are for nothing. The beer reticulation system is my one of one percenters.

How we make our pubs so profitable

People often ask how we're able to take a pub, buy it at a good price and then resell or revalue it a short time later at such a high price or valuation—it's because of the little things I'm mentioning here. A rebrand, a refresh, a coat of paint, new systems, new staff, new menus, new events, new promotions. It's not brain surgery, but it takes time and attention to detail to get it all aligned. It's about vision too. I can walk into a pub and see instantly what its potential is. That 'blink' moment Malcom Gladwell talks about in his book *Blink* is what I'm referring to here: that busted lightbulb, that broken door: I see it all, instantly, and can tell that the owner has become bored or is worn down with the workload of keeping it all together.

Everyone's welcome

It's not just important to do the little things right, you need to do the right thing—for your customers, your staff and your suppliers—and if you do that, it will come back to benefit you. Maybe not immediately, but in the long term it will pay off.

For example, when someone comes into our pub and orders a glass of water, and nothing else, and then breaks out their laptop, phone, mini speaker and head buds, and proceeds to sit on that glass of water for hours, without ordering so much as a mocha, the temptation would be to say, 'Pack up your bags and nick off. You're taking up valuable space that paying customers want to use'. Tempting, but no. Our values are that everyone is welcome, no matter who they are, how much they spend or how long they stay. As such, we ensure that not only do they get their glass of water, but that the glass of water comes with cracked ice, a slice of lemon and a coaster, and an offer to top the water up every quarter hour.

Does it cost us? Sure, but it's the right thing to do. We treat all our customers the same, no matter what. Maybe that glass of water, delivered with style and a smile, is the one nice thing that person has experienced that day, that week or that year; maybe that glass of water will one day lead to that customer coming back and ordering a glass of wine, a meal and more.

Treat everyone with respect – except rock stars

In return for making everyone welcome, we ask that our customers treat our staff and venue with respect. I have zero tolerance for anyone in any venue feeling threatened, unsafe or intimidated. Has this policy cost me? Sure — both financially and physically. But it's the right thing to do. I've never forgotten one incident. It was 1995. I was working in a bar called The King's Head in Earls Court in London, the suburb of choice for party-loving Aussies, Kiwis and South Africans. The King's Head was an early version of a sports bar with posters of the Wallabies, All Blacks and Springbok rugby teams plastered all over the timber walls. The place could get pretty wild at night, but being a party-loving, rugby-mad Aussie, I felt right at home.

I was on my day off, just stopping off to pick up some paperwork at the pub and to say hello to the locals. I noticed two men in the front bar. They looked unkempt, unshaven, and were wearing torn, dirty jeans, cursing like crazy and chugging back the beers like there was no tomorrow. One of them stood up, wobbly on his feet, leaned over the bar and started to pour himself a drink. The bar waitress, Sally, an Aussie girl, who I had hired just one week earlier, asked him to stop, but that just set him off. Sally had fingers jabbed in her direction and F-bombs and C-words yelled loudly at her, among other names. I wasn't having that.

I nodded to my boss, Adam, a big Brisbane boy built like a brick shithouse, to prepare for a 'staged exit' as we called it in the business. He knew what to do. He quietly removed the empty glasses on the bar so they couldn't be used as weapons, and then gave me the signal. I stood up, removed the glasses of beer they were drinking, grabbed them by the scruff of their shabby shirts, hoisted them off their barstools, frog marched them to the door, and threw them out into the alley. They landed hard against the adjoining wall, shocked and confused at this unexpected turn of events, wondering what had happened and what had hit them.

One of my regulars, who watched all this unfold, said, 'That was a brave move'.

'Why?' I asked.

'Do you know who they were?'

'No.'

'Only the biggest band in the world right now.'

'And who would that be?'

'I *believe* that was Oasis.'

I just laughed. They might be wondering what wall they hit, but I had no regrets at all about my actions. I might have lost a bit of business that day (they were drinking a lot!) and I may have lost bragging rights for hosting the biggest band in the world in my bar, but their behaviour, language and attitude were way out of line, even by rock-star standards. I don't care who you are or what you do, if you're in my bar you treat everyone with respect. Throwing them out was the right thing to do.

A lot can and does go wrong in a pub, most of which you may not see, thank goodness, but in trying to do the little things right, and do the right things, on a constant basis, you increase your chances of getting the bigger things right too, like making a profit, creating a loyal clientele and building a cool brand.

Mind over matter

Mahatma Gandhi famously said, 'I have so much to accomplish today that I must meditate for two hours instead of one'.

We're all busy these days and it's tempting to skip important routines that keep us in good working order.

Gandhi knew what many of us are slowly cottoning onto: calming your mind is critical to succeeding in life. Be it sport, business or your personal relationships, responding in the moment is the key to success. You can see it in action on the football field every week. Why is it that the top football players, who've been playing football for decades and can kick a goal from 50 metres out during training, fail to kick a goal in a high-pressure game a few metres out? It's not their foot that causes issues; it's their focus. Their attention has gone to the last umpiring decision that went against them, the voice in the crowd, the voice of the coach or just the voice in their head. When we're under stress, we end up swimming in the oceans of our own mind, with too many thoughts and too many distractions. It's why most major football clubs of all codes (and other sports) now routinely engage mindfulness coaches. They know that the difference between winning and losing is not so much about what's happening on the field—it's what happening in the player's head. Training the mind to perform under pressure is the last frontier and the coaches who realise this know that winning and losing is often all in managing the mind.

It's the same with business. We take knocks all the time—a trusted team member leaves us, a marketing campaign falls flat, a real estate development deal falls over, the government increases a tax—you name it, we've been through it. It's part of being in the game of business. But it's the business owners who can take a deep breath, connect with their higher power and access their inner wisdom who will win out. Meditation is the key to transcending these emotional troughs, keeping perspective and dealing with difficult times.

WHEN THE GOING GETS TOUGH

I'm old enough to remember when the Goods and Services Tax (GST) was introduced into Australia. The logistics of implementing this were complicated and many small-business owners found it so overwhelming, they just pulled the pin, sold their business or walked away. They couldn't cope with the complexity of what the government was asking them to do. They were frightened of the impact it would have on their business and decided they'd rather leave than deal with it.

Fast forward to now and the GST is just a standard part of what we do and it's no big deal. Yes, it was a pain in the arse at the time and there was much confusion about what incurred the tax and what didn't. (Just google 'John Hewson, Birthday Cake' and you'll know what I mean.)

But we knew the logistical headache of implementing it wouldn't last forever. I often wonder if those business owners who walked away all those years ago now wish they'd tried harder to push through it. If they had been able to calm their mind and get some perspective on the future to help them get through those difficult early days, where would they be now?

Change is constant in every business, and it's the business owners who can manage the change who will succeed.

The benefits of meditation

Having the ability to still the mind, review the situation with a cool head and make decisions from a place of strength, rather than fear, is what meditation can do for a business owner. It can help you 'buy' a bit of mental preparation time so that when something happens you don't react in the moment, say or do the wrong thing and then live to regret it.

Mindfulness creates the mental space you need—maybe just a few seconds—to see the situation clearly, decide on the best course of action, minimise whatever emotional current is running through your brain and come up with a response that is right for that moment.

The 20/30 rule

We all know the Pareto Principle—80 per cent of anything comes from 20 per cent of effort. When it comes to setting yourself up for a productive day, I have an adjustment to that concept. I call it the 20/30 rule and it's all about the morning ritual. I truly believe most days end badly because they start badly. Don't make that rookie mistake. One of my favourite authors is Robin Sharma, author of *The Monk Who Sold His Ferrari*. His book *The 5AM Club* shows why the morning ritual is so important, and I couldn't agree more.

Here's how I structure my morning ritual upon waking:

- 20 minutes planning

- 30 minutes reading

- 20 minutes meditation

- 30 minutes weights

- 20 minutes ice bath (I set my swimming pool temperature to eight degrees to create 'ice bath' conditions. When I didn't have a swimming pool, I just had a really cold bath or shower.)

- 30 minutes sauna.

Yes, it's 150 minutes, which may seem a lot of time to dedicate to a morning ritual, especially if you've got a young family and a bustling household. But out of the 1440 minutes we get every day, surely dedicating 10 per cent of your time to setting the day up right is a good use of it. As Gandhi asserted, the busier you are, the more time you need to centre yourself to stay strong.

Meditation has been my 'go to' secret weapon for many years now. My morning ritual is fixed and only an emergency or an inconvenient travel schedule can throw me off. Sure, it's a big hit of time out of my day, but on the days I don't do it, the day invariably goes poorly. Call me superstitious (I'm not) but I know that the way I start the day tends to inform how I finish the day.

Mechanics of the mind

If your car isn't working, you take it to the mechanic. Our minds are no different. If we're not feeling great in the head, and meditation isn't helping, we need to take ourselves to a 'mechanic of the mind': a psychologist, psychiatrist, GP or social worker.

I take my mental health seriously. After a serious family crisis involving my oldest daughter, Holly, I knew that I was careering dangerously off course and I could feel a train wreck coming on. I could have soldiered on and pushed through, trying to deal with it myself, but I knew the pressure was taking hold and I could not see a solution. With the help of my wife Fidelma, who was a senior nurse unit manager of a private psychiatric clinic, we found a counsellor. I met with the counsellor on a number of occasions and found her advice to be invaluable. The experience was so helpful, I took the whole family to see her because we all needed help; we all needed to heal from the trauma Holly experienced. It was a wise decision because it gave us the tools we needed to heal. We still go every couple of years as a family; it's a way of 'taking the temperature' and we're a stronger, more close-knit family for it.

What I've also come to appreciate is that my children now know that seeing a counsellor is not something to be embarrassed about but something to move towards. Just as we aren't embarrassed to take our car to the motor mechanic, we shouldn't be embarrassed to take ourselves to the mind mechanic.

Help staff help themselves

The days of 'command and control' as a management strategy are well and truly over. If we employ staff and want to give them autonomy to make important decisions, we can't be second guessing them every step of the way. Sure, they'll make mistakes, but that's part and parcel of being a business owner. I want to give my team a tool for helping them be more resilient so they can weather the various crises that will come their way. We know that anxiety and depression are on the rise and even the seemingly most well-adjusted people (myself included) can be susceptible to mental health issues. It's predicted that by 2025 it will affect over 25 per cent of Australians. That's a hefty number. Look around your family. If there are more than four people in it, one of you is likely to be part of that statistic.

My staff are an extension of my family so I've created an initiative called the Employment Assistance Program (EAP). We fund our staff to attend up to three visits to a counsellor of their choice so that if they're feeling lacklustre or down, they can get the help they need at no cost to them. They can also do it on work time. If you help them help themselves, you'll generally find that when the chips are down, they'll help you too.

Summing up ...

1. Success has its origins in decades past. Work on the micro goals and you'll attain the macro goals.

2. Identify the things that matter. Some things don't make a difference. Others do. Find them.

3. Don't just rely on instinct to make decisions. Collect the right data and use it to make informed decisions.

4. Connect with others in your industry so you can keep up to date with benchmarks, standards, industry intelligence and best practice.

5. Treat everyone well, and the same, no matter who they are.

6. If things go wrong, don't panic or walk away. It will (almost always) get better.

7. Take your mental health seriously. Don't be afraid to seek help if you need it.

8. Take time to create a morning ritual that sets you up for the day.

9. Start your day strong and you're likely to end your day strong.

Part II
BUILD

You want to build your business, scale it up and create a repeatable business model that makes money while you sleep, so it's time to get serious about principles, processes and procedures.

Identifying your passion is important, but making a profit from that passion is what you now need to focus on. Finding what you love and systematising it so that others can take over without your direct involvement is the key to growth.

When you're in 'build' mode, you may be buying more properties, taking over other businesses, hiring more staff, leasing warehouses or bringing on new investors.

In short, if you want to maximise your profit and minimise your risk, you'll need to think like a business owner, not like a business operator.

It took me 30 years to become an overnight success. In part II, I unpack all that, document the journey and lay bare the success formulas that helped me achieve such incredible results in quite a short time, plus the mistakes I've made along the way that cost me dearly. I hope you can learn from both.

CHAPTER 5

Build your confidence

> **For a man to conquer himself is the first and noblest of all victories.**
>
> *Plato*

When I raised $1 million in eight hours to buy The Rutherford, and turned it into a roaring success, I learned a few lessons along the way. Lessons like how to raise money quickly, how to do it under pressure and how not to make assumptions. All critical lessons if you don't want to get sued, go bankrupt or lose control of your business before you've even started.

I also learned that I had a passion for turning under-performing pubs into profit-making machines. That sense of breathing life back into a grand old pub that had seen better days really excited me, so in 2015, feeling buoyed by this early success and eager to replicate it, I launched my 'pub fund'.

Taking on a considerable level of debt to buy The Rutherford (at a purchase price of $4.2 million) was a big step for me, and a significant risk, but I was willing to do it as I've always lived by the motto, 'You've got one life and you're a long time dead'—so you may as well rip in, crack on and have a red-hot go. I could see the current pub owner had lost a bit of interest in the property and was letting things slide, and I knew I could restore it to its former glory. Importantly, the local community was super supportive, loved a good pint and parma and would be loyal to us if we looked after them.

We got stuck in really quickly, dug into the financials, did the little things right, worked hard to improve our profit margins and, six months later, had it valued at a cool $5 million. We then did what we always do with our pubs: gave it a mighty rebrand and renovation. Three months later, it was revalued at $5.2 million. All up, we increased the value of the pub by $1 million in just one year.

People often ask, 'Surely a renovation can't generate that much extra equity in such a short time?'. Yes, it can—especially when the reno is done well. In practice it's pretty tricky because you have to keep what the locals loved about the old pub, but inject a new energy and passion into the new pub. You can't change too much, but you do need to make changes. We focused on making our pubs look amazing, but worked really hard on improving the margins and that all came back to our principles, processes and procedures. We changed the menu and the drinks list, held more events, built better relationships with the suppliers, secured great rebates from our partners (which enabled us to keep our prices reasonable), retained the high-performing team members (moved those on who weren't) and provided the locals with everything they were accustomed to, but bigger and better. That, in short, was how we maximised our valuations every time.

If you don't ask, you don't get

The investors in the pub fund were delighted with the results we delivered. They received a capital gain and a really strong cash return. They were so delighted, they said, 'Hey Steve, when are you going to buy another pub? We want to invest again'.

'Great,' I thought. 'Now I just need to find another pub to buy!'

I approached an old friend of mine, Craig Higgins, who had been a part-owner in a pub called The Lakeside Village Tavern in Port Stephens, NSW for years. He and I had shared many a late-night laugh over the years and I was looking forward to catching up with him. We sat down for a beer and he said, 'Steve, my business partners want to sell, but I don't. I'd like to slow down a little but I don't want to give the game away entirely. What advice have you got for me?'

My 'hunting' instinct kicked in and I said, 'How about I buy the pub from you but you stay on as an investor? You can get all the fun of having a pub without the work.'

He said, 'I'm in!'

What a scoop! Now I just had to find the money to pay for it. The potential was exciting. Not only had I found a pub to buy, I also found an investor to help me fund it: a valuable mentor and seasoned veteran who would help me negotiate the new acquisition and stay on so we could hit the ground running. The deal was a masterstroke and a great reminder that if you want something, you need to ask for it. If I hadn't asked Craig if he wanted to sell, I wouldn't have bought The Lakeside Village Tavern today. You've got to have a crack!

The Lakeside Tavern, Port Stephens.

When it rains, it pours (beers)

Not long after this conversation, I attended a community event at my son's footy club. The organisers knew I was coming so they sat me next to a pub broker, which was very thoughtful of them. We got chatting and he said, 'There's an outstanding pub about to hit the market. The location is awesome, the chef is world class and the locals are rusted on. The owners would prefer to sell it off market, so if you're interested let me know and I'll set up a meeting'.

I didn't have to think twice. I had investors lined up wanting to buy into my next pub, and my energy and appetite to acquire more pubs was growing. I did my due diligence and the numbers stacked up so I said, 'Yep. I'm in!'

The total price for the two pubs? $15.65 million. No problem. Now all I had to do was find $15.65 million. I wasn't going to make the mistake I had made earlier and commit to a purchase without securing the funds first. I'd definitely learned my lesson there.

Like numbers? Here's a few

Having previously raised $1 million in one day, it would, technically speaking, only take me 15 days to raise $15 million, but I decided to err on the side of caution and get as long a settlement as I could so that I didn't give myself so much stress. I opted for a 90-day settlement.

By the way, the reason I'm sharing with you my tactics for raising money is because I want you to know that anyone can do it—and it applies to any business you might be buying. I know it's easy for me to say that now, as I've already 'been there, done that', but when I started, I was no different to you or anyone else. I had to learn how to research a project, value it, find investors, pitch the deal, secure it, do the paperwork, build the pub, make a profit and then do it all over again.

When you're sitting in front of an investor and you're sweating bullets trying to justify why they should give you a million bucks, you're on your own and only you can make it happen.

Structuring the deal and sourcing the funds

The bank was so happy with our previous achievements, they loaned us 65 per cent of $15.65 million (around $10 million), based on the value of the two pubs combined.

That, plus a loan of 65 per cent of $5.2 million (around $3 million), which was the value of The Rutherford (the first pub we bought in 2015 as part of our pub fund) helped me reach $13 million.

I had already sourced $2.4 million of investor money, and The Rutherford had increased in value by $1 million since I purchased it, so that gave me another $3.4 million.

So, $13 million plus $3.4 million gave me $16.4 million. All up, I needed $21 million. Just $4.6 million to go! Nearly there. I went back to one of my original investors, the ones who had helped me raise $1 million in eight hours, and they invested another $2 million and introduced me to some other investors. Beauty. Only $2.6 million to go.

Taking time out

Knowing I had 90 days to raise this capital, I decided to take some time out to get some inspiration, so I headed over to England for a few weeks to attend my godson Adam's christening (his father, Daniel, is one of my closest mates who helped me launch my backyard beer garden, and has been a significant advisor and investor since) and to undertake a course I'd been super keen to complete. It was a certificate in marketing and entrepreneurship at The London School of Economics and Political Science. As part of the course, we got to pitch to our classmates so I took the opportunity to pitch my investment ideas to them. While they didn't invest, they gave me some invaluable advice on how to tweak the pitch to make it more appealing. I also got some great tax advice from some Russian bankers who attended the course. They were kind of intimidating gals, the kind you see in the Russia Mafia or a James Bond movie, but they were super smart and provided a global perspective that was invaluable.

While I was knocking back vodka at late-night bars with my new-found Russian friends, my trusty accountant Annette Pulbrook and board member Tim Wearne were hard at work back at home, drumming up investors for me and sorting out the documentation. The paperwork was enormous, with dozens of contracts to review and sign. I personally am fond of numbers so these documents don't faze me, but if you're not that way inclined, you need to find a good accountant and lawyer who can step you through the process. It's critical you don't sign something that can come back to bite you on the butt, so take this step seriously and do the due diligence needed to protect yourself and your investors.

This time around, the bank was very happy to provide me with funds, and by day 80—10 days out from the deadline—we had raised the $15.65 million we needed. All up the fund was now worth $21 million.

How we grew the pub fund from $400 000 to $100 million

Our pub fund, valued at a mere $400 000 in 2015, had—with the purchase of The Lakeside Village Tavern and The Duke Hotel—grown to $21 million by 2016.

Ocean View Hotel, Urunga NSW.

We had the portfolio revalued in 2017 at $23 million. We also bought a lease on the Ocean View Hotel in the same year. This new valuation was important as it meant we could get an 'interest only' loan, which meant we could reinvest more funds back into the pub and provide my investors with a better return.

We were on a roll.

In 2018 we bought a long lease (30 years) on Finnian's Irish Tavern Port Macquarie.

We'd had the pub fund for three years now and decided it was a good time to look around and review our options. Should we keep growing? Sell some assets? We were keen to expand into new offerings and diversify, so when we found The Sea Breeze Hotel—a cracking pub in Nelson Bay, about 200 kilometres north of Sydney that had 17 water-view accommodation units on the title—we did our due diligence (which didn't take long) and bought it. Dan, the agent selling the pub, was the same agent who had sold us The Duke Hotel. He always had great assets to sell and was good at putting good deals together.

To raise the funds for this purchase of The Sea Breeze Hotel we sold The Rutherford (remembering we paid $4.2 million for it) for a handsome $6.5 million. This covered the costs of the Sea Breeze and gave our investors a tidy return.

Diversity is important for any business, but extremely important for pubs like mine because we're susceptible to so many variables outside our control. For example, when COVID-19 came along, our bars and restaurants were hit hard, but our bottle shops fired up. When winter comes, the bottle shops taper off but the football crowds in the front bar make up for it. If COVID-19 has taught us anything, it's that we need to be flexible, keep our options open and have multiple streams of income.

In 2019, I bought The Kent pub in Hamilton, New South Wales from my family (we had bought it as a family in 2002). We took a breather in 2020 (hello COVID!) and in 2021 bought the Imperial Hotel and the Harrington Hotel, which took the market capitalisation of the pubs under management to over $100 million.

My capital-raising efforts started out on pretty shaky ground. I was inexperienced and naïve and that put me in some pretty stressful situations. But just a few years later, as you can see, I had the hang of it and realised that while it was hard work and required incredible focus and attention to detail, I loved doing it and was good at it. If this was work, give me more of it!

After all, where else can you do what you love, bring people together, show them a great time, make money and give your investors a chance to enjoy their investment by coming into the pub and seeing it in action? I was thirsty for more success. I just needed to find more pubs, and the money to buy them with.

When you're on a good thing, stick to it

Investing in shares and commercial property might be profitable, but for most investors, they're generally digital transactions and mostly clinical in execution. That's why my investors kept coming back. After all, what's not to like about inviting your mates down for a cold one after work to *your* pub? That sense of ownership played a big role in securing investors. They loved the fact my pubs were bricks and mortar: something they could see, feel, experience and be a part of. Not only were they making money from their investment, but they were having fun doing it. I always invite investors to the pub to celebrate when a deal is completed. We dine like kings and have the time of our lives. These celebrations take me back to when I was 17 years old, building my first accidental pub in my parents' backyard. Here I am doing it again—just bigger, bolder and with better wine!

Buying pubs has become my obsession.

Finding investors was no longer a problem

Our investors loved what we were doing, understood our need to spread the risk and appreciated the effort we undertook. When you're offering a track record of 12 per cent cash returns, paid quarterly, with 15 per cent appreciation over the lifetime of the investment, you know you're doing something right and so do your investors, which is why they started to come knocking on our door—and we welcomed them in with open arms.

For reasons like this, I no longer struggled to find investors. They liked our multi-tiered business model, our well-trained team, and my honesty and straight-shooting style, and they really liked the fact I'd been knocking around pubs for decades. There hasn't been a job I haven't done in a pub so I could answer almost any question they had about running one. My dad invested in pubs. My great-uncle owned pubs. I had worked in pubs all over the world as a barman, doorman, licensee and manager—and I have worked for some of the best pub owners in the world, who taught me everything they knew. I started at the bottom and worked my way to the top. I cooked, cleaned, washed glasses, changed the lightbulbs, wrote the menus, bought the stock, poured the beers, negotiated the leases, dealt with the authorities—and much more. When it came to pubs, I knew a fair bit about them and what it took to run them.

Our secret weapon: the multi-factor model (MFM)

Why were we so good at buying pubs and making them profitable?

While it might look like I was buying any pub I could find, my methodology for asset acquisition is very stringent. I don't put my finger in the air and wait for the breeze to blow to tell me what to do. Over the years, I've developed a very sophisticated modelling system called the multi-factor model (MFM). This spreadsheet evaluates a series of weighted categories, which enables us to complete complex due diligence processes very quickly. Each category gets scored, which creates a final number that tells us whether to proceed with the deal or not. The factors we assess include location, potential size, speed to victory, risk, financial feasibility and, most importantly, the team required for success. The process requires careful analysis and attention to detail, but it has become an integral tool that helps us determine what to buy, when, where, for how much, and what performance we can expect from it. It's become the touchstone for my team when making major decisions and it's enabled us to create a pub empire that outperforms the average pub across almost all categories.

Every time we assess a new property, we just plug in the data, adjust the weightings accordingly, score each property and quickly determine its potential. My team and trusted advisors value this model because this software contains the personal intellectual property I've accumulated over 30 years in the business and creates a decision-making framework for a process I have always done instinctively. It's our secret weapon.

Summing up ...

1. If you want to scale a business, you need to get serious about systems.

2. People can't read your mind. Ask for what you want. If you don't ask, you don't get.

3. Diversify your income streams to spread the risk and protect yourself from downturns in the market.

4. Understand the factors that impact on profitability.

5. Create a framework for decision making so that you don't rely on instinct to make important financial choices.

CHAPTER 6
Build your team

> An arch consists of two weaknesses which, leaning on each other, become a strength.
>
> *Leonardo da Vinci*

I spoke at a business event a while back. At the end of the speech, a man got up and asked me a question: 'What are the top three most important elements in running a business?' he asked.

'People, people, people,' I said.

He thought I was joking, but I wasn't. That advice doesn't make for good 'copy' or a shareable meme on social media, but ignore it at your peril. Whether you're a one-person band or a multinational, if you don't focus on your people, you're cactus, and when I say 'people', I don't just mean staff: I mean suppliers, customers and everyone else in the supply chain.

How to build a loyal team

I have over 350 staff on my team, and a lot of them have been with me for more than 20 years. That's loyalty. They've been with me from the get-go when funds were low and debt was high and we all had to pitch in and dig deep to make the bloody thing work. I've had fights, fires and floods, even deaths in my pubs, and yet my team have stuck with me through thick and thin. I've learned a few things along the way on how to hire (and keep) good staff. If you're about to hire staff and don't want to make a mistake, take a look at some of the strategies I've used that have worked well for me.

But first, before you hire anyone, it's worth discovering how much your staff are really costing you. I mean *really* costing you. It's probably more than you think.

HOW MUCH ARE YOUR STAFF REALLY COSTING YOU?

If you had an investment property worth $1 million, you'd take good care of it, wouldn't you? You'd paint the walls, fix the broken window, mow the lawn and more.

If you had a staff member worth $1 million, you'd take care of them too, wouldn't you? You'd care what they thought, invest in them, try to bring out their best. Because the reality is, if you have a staff member on your team whom you're paying more than $50 000 a year, they're actually valued at $1 million a year. 'How does that work?' I hear you ask.

Here's how we calculate the value of a staff member.

If you were to borrow $1 million from a bank, at 5 per cent interest, you'd pay back $50 000 in interest per year. So, for every $50 000 you spend on wages, that converts to $1 million in capital value, which means if one staff member is paid $50 000, they are actually worth $1 million to you.

If you were responsible for maintaining a million-dollar asset, would that change the way you treat that person? That's how valuable a $50 000 wage earner is costing you. If you knew how much that staff member really cost you, would you treat them a little differently and work a bit harder to keep them? Now that you know how much each staff member is worth, does that change the way you see them? It should.

Hire slow, fire fast

You don't need me to tell you that hiring staff is one of the riskiest and most expensive aspects of running a business. A bad 'hire' can go so wrong so easily and break a business.

The old phrase, 'Hire in haste, regret at leisure' is true. I take my time when hiring as the cost of getting it wrong is enormous. It goes without saying that hiring people with the same values as you is critical to success. People don't always wear their values on their sleeve, which makes it hard to see what makes people tick; first impressions aren't always right and what people say at an interview and what they do when they get the job are often two very different things.

When hiring new staff, especially for important roles, I conduct multiple interviews with applicants before I offer them a job and ask them a wide range of questions (not necessarily related to the job at hand) before I make a decision.

Very few job interview processes, tests or quizzes can truly reveal a person's character. Having a meal with them can. Breaking bread at a dinner table is one of the most fruitful environments for revealing the underlying nature of a person. This may seem superficial or flippant, but I learn a lot from the experience.

I've developed a process over the years for how to interview people. I call it the LOAN process. It's pretty simple but powerful at the same time. I simply:

- *Listen* to what's being said (without interrupting)

- *Observe* what's going on (watching for both verbal and non-verbal language)

- *Ask* lots of questions (without making assumptions or judgements)

- *Note* it all down (for review and reflection later on).

I apply that process when I'm having a meal with them. Here's what I observe during the meal:

- I watch their actions.

- I watch their interactions.

- I watch what they order.

Let me expand on this.

Watch their actions

I'm not looking for anything in particular during the meal, but eating is an activity that subconsciously reveals a great deal about a person. For example, I take note of how they use the cutlery. I don't personally care how they hold their knife or fork, or if they know the difference between a soup spoon and a dessert spoon, but the way they use the cutlery tells me volumes about their education, upbringing, demographic and more. Sometimes hiring people who don't know what spoon is which is an asset because a pub is an egalitarian place that attracts people from all walks of life, and having a staff member who comes from a working-class background and can hold their own in a boisterous environment is worth its weight in gold.

Watch their interactions

Having a meal helps me observe how they interact with the people around them. For example, are they polite and respectful to the wait staff, or are they dismissive, aloof and cold? Do they engage with the people around them, make eye contact, smile and spark up a casual conversation, or do they keep to themselves and speak only when spoken to? Do they treat everyone equally, irrespective of where they sit in the pecking order? I'm looking for indications for how they'll fit in with the team. Will they pitch in and step up when the going gets tough? Will they offer to help out when it's not technically 'their job'? Will they upset the team dynamic? Pubs are nothing if not about team work. Nothing gets done in isolation. If the meals aren't ready, the wait staff cop it. If the glasses are dirty, the bar staff cop it. Everyone needs to be hands on at all times, ready to help others when they need it. I need a team player.

Watch what they order

I watch to see what they order. I'm not fussed what they eat, but their choice conveys meaning. Do they order the most expensive item on the menu or do they show restraint? Do they order something healthy or indulge in a feast of fatty foods? Are they thankful for the meal or do they take it for granted? I don't judge them, I just notice them; the mosaic of who they are begins to form and a clearer picture of who this person is emerges. The meal may only last an hour, but it reveals more than a week of formal interviews ever could.

Don't hire rock stars

I've hired a few 'rock star' employees in my time. You know the sort: good looking, charming, persuasive. They dazzle everyone with their aura of glamour and, for a while, everything is sweet. But then everyone gets used to them and their beauty premium wears off and we're left with nothing but their work ethic, personality and values—and that's when their real character emerges. When you're born beautiful, or charming, you get given a lot without having to work for it, which can breed laziness and a sense of entitlement. Not always of course, but sometimes.

This work ethic shows up in the little things. For example, they take a smoko when the bar is going nuts and the barman could do with an extra hand; they don't pick up the crayons in the kids' play area because, technically, 'it's not their job'; they arrive a few minutes late and leave a few minutes early, and give the bare minimum in notice if they're sick, which they are—often.

Then, after a few months of hard(ly) working, when their true nature has been noticed by others (and seen as wanting), they slide off into the sunset, ready to drizzle their glitter on the next unsuspecting employer who'll be bedazzled by their beauty and charm. But the damage they do to the team doesn't leave with them. The remaining team is left unsettled, their loyalties have been tested and the experience has brought out the worst in everyone.

Be wary of hiring rock stars.

Check references

This sounds obvious, but you'd be amazed at how few employers read resumes thoroughly or ask to speak to referees. If you're to minimise the risk of making a bad hire, you must do all that. Hiring the wrong staff is just too costly and a simple referee check can give you the information needed to make a wise decision.

One strategy that has served me well over the years is I take a moment to look for the gaps on their resume and ask them what they were doing in that time. The candidate left those gaps for a reason and you will want to know what they were doing in those 'gap years'. That will tell you as much as the rest of the resume. I like to give interviewees the chance to tell me what really happened at their last workplace. I want them to feel comfortable knowing that I don't automatically take the side of an employer. On the occasion I've been able to talk to their last employer, I've come away thinking: 'Yeah, if I worked for them, I would have resigned too'.

How to keep staff

Now you've found good staff, you want to keep them. That requires effort. Good staff will always be head hunted so you need to be on your A-game to ensure they stay loyal to you.

Firstly, get them involved in your decision-making process so they understand the 'why' behind your thinking. Ask for their advice, listen to what they suggest, take it seriously and provide them with the resources they need to get the job done. More importantly, agree on the outcome you're seeking, and let them achieve it in their own way. When your team are clear on the 'what' and the 'why', they will take care of the 'how' and deliver you a result that far exceeds what you could have expected if you'd told them how to do it.

Sharing the success

I often get asked how I keep my staff so loyal. I work at it, but there are some basic strategies you can implement that make it easier to achieve. For example, when I hired Ricci-lee, my Marketing and Operations Manager, I offered her a share in the business via the framework known as the Employee Share Options Program (ESOP). I don't offer it to everybody on the team, obviously, but when I find good staff who have a role to play in the oversight of the entire portfolio, it makes sense to incentivise them to work hard and stay loyal.

HOW OUR EMPLOYEE SHARE OPTIONS PROGRAM (ESOP) WORKS

In 2015, my pub empire was worth $400 000. By 2019, it was worth over $63 million. That kind of growth creates casualties; my health and personal life were two of them. I knew I couldn't keep going at that pace. But I was totally absorbed in what I was doing and thrilled with the impact (and the profit) we were making.

I thought, *I need to hire someone to help me run this ... but who?* The person would need a blend of marketing and operational skills, be able to work hard and fast, deal with multiple projects, oversee a large team of people, be on top of the detail and do it all with good humour. So it wasn't an easy role to fill and despite multiple interviews with high-calibre applicants, the role remained unfilled.

And then along came Ricci-Lee. I met Ricci-Lee when she worked for the Southern Cross Radio/Austereo Group. She was a dynamic sales rep and she'd come in each month to help me develop media campaigns to promote my network of businesses. She was a force of nature: upbeat, proactive, endlessly creative and untiring in her intent to deliver unparalleled customer service to me and my team.

When I offered her the role, we designed the employment contract together and she was very open about what she could bring to the

(continued)

business, but equally important, what she could not. I was candid too. This way, both her and my needs were fulfilled. Co-creating an employment contract with the employee makes sense. After all, if the employee doesn't like or agree with what they're meant to do or achieve, they're unlikely to comply with it, let alone surpass it.

The nuts and bolts of an ESOP

The ESOP program I created for Ricci-Lee was pretty straightforward. For illustrative purposes, let's assume I give Ricci-Lee $50 000 worth of 'units': she now effectively 'owes' the company $50 000 for those units. The more money we make, the quicker her 'debt' gets paid off, the quicker she owns a share in the business and the quicker she receives the requisite benefits that come with ownership (e.g. returns, dividends).

It's a bit more complicated than that, but in essence, the plan is designed to give an employee some 'skin in the game': to share with them the success of the business and give them a sense of ownership so they don't leave. It works well.

Like all legal agreements, an ESOP needs to be carefully designed to suit you and your staff member. By all means, download a template from the internet to get you started, but you'll need to protect yourself and incorporate aspects such as a 'good leave' (when they leave on good terms) and the reverse, a 'bad leave' (when they don't), so speak to your lawyer and accountant as there are very specific clauses you will need to include.

Developing an intrapreneurial culture

If you wandered into one of my pubs, you'd find a diverse group of people running it. You'd see a mighty Pacific Islander on the door, a mum-of-three managing the café, a tattooed hipster making coffee and a pot-bellied ex-policeman pouring beers in the bar. I like hiring people who are wildly different from me. It keeps things interesting, opens my mind and forces me to consider multiple points of view. It also pays off in unexpected but profitable ways.

The nature of pub life is that it attracts seasonal (and diverse) workers so we have to work hard to keep our staff happy. Helping them achieve their goals under our roof benefits us both.

Unleash your team's passion for your profit

We've all heard about how important it is to develop entrepreneurial culture in our organisations, but the smart money is on developing an intrapreneurial culture. This is where you unleash the power and passion of your staff to help them (and you) achieve mutually rewarding goals at the same time. Hiring diverse people helps you attract a wide range of skillsets and perspectives, which sets the foundation for creating an intrapreneurial culture.

HOW TO FOSTER AN INTRAPRENEURIAL CULTURE

'How can you tell if someone's a vegan?'

'Don't worry. They'll tell you.'

That was the joke Luca told me when he was being interviewed as a chef for one of my pubs. He got the job because he's an awesome chef and a terrific team player, and he has a great sense of humour (for a vegan). He couldn't have been less like me. He was single, 28, tall, thin, with a shaved head and multiple piercings through the nose, the lips and possibly other places that I don't even want to contemplate.

He had been with me for a year and was a model employee, but I could sense he was getting bored and was looking around for a new challenge, or a new job. I didn't want him to leave but didn't really have any other role for him to step into at that time. I don't like losing staff as it's expensive to find new people and time consuming to train them, so when I could see Luca losing interest (in subtle ways that my robust reporting system detected long before anyone else spotted it), I stepped in to find out what was going on.

I said, 'Luca, let me buy you lunch (did I mention I like to have meetings over a meal?) and let's have a chat about what we can do to keep you here

(continued)

and stay loyal to us'. When we sat down, I asked him, 'I can sense you're losing interest in your work. I want to work with you to see if there's something we can do to help you get that spring back in your step'.

We talked and ate and I asked him a bunch of questions about his life outside of work. The one about, 'What do you like cooking at home?' piqued his interest.

'Anything vegan,' he said.

'What like?' I asked?

He rattled off a range of dishes: red curry chickpea dahl, spicy Chinese eggplant with Szechuan sauce, crispy quinoa and beetroot wraps, Peruvian burritos with creamy black beans, and more. I'm a dyed-in-the-wool meat-eater and even I liked the sound of those dishes!

'Luca, if you could wave a magic wand over the job you currently have, what would help you stay motivated and engaged?'

Without blinking, as if he'd already thought this through, he said, 'I'd love to replace the menu we have with a totally vegan menu'.

Now my first thought was, *Shit! That's not gonna happen! What about the wagyu my regulars love? The spag bol that sells its socks off? The chicken schnitty with chips and pepper sauce?* Food sales are an important part of our profit profile so I wouldn't — couldn't — take a punt on a vegan hipster messing with my margins. I had to compromise.

'I love where you're going with this, Luca, and I really want to give you the opportunity to express your passion here under my roof, so how about we compromise? We keep the current menu, but you can create another vegan menu and we'll run them alongside each other for a month to see how it goes. If it goes well, we keep it. If it doesn't, at least we know we had a crack and tried something new. What do you think?'

He sat up straight, smiled and said, 'When can I start?'

'Today, mate, today.' And with that, he went back to the kitchen and started scribbling on a pad, designing his new vegan menu. He was buzzing. I was buzzing. I'd convinced this wonderful young man to stay, not by asking him to, but by listening, observing and asking him what he needed. If you have the courage to ask people what they want, people will generally tell you.

Luca got to work, weaved his magic around the vegan menu and, within weeks of launching, we increased profits in the dining room by over 18 per cent. It was remarkable.

It gets better.

Not only did we increase profits in the dining room, we increased profits throughout the entire pub. Why? Well, it's called the law of unintended consequences. What I didn't know is that there is a massive underground network of vegans who, it would appear, all know each other! Yeah. Go figure. They have their own dedicated Facebook pages and Instagram pages and love to share what's hot and happening in the vegan world.

Within days, we had hordes of vegans descending on us to try out our new menu. This network of very switched-on, socially conscious souls took it upon themselves to market our business for us: they couldn't wait to tell their friends, and anyone who would listen, that this regional pub, which used to specialise in spaghetti Bolognese and chicken schnitzel, was now the go-to place for all things vegan. And guess what? Vegans drink—a lot—and bet on the football, and have grandmas who like to have afternoon tea on a Saturday afternoon at the pub, and cousins who play soccer and need an after-game venue to celebrate/commiserate, and sisters who need a nice venue in which to get married.

Yes, that young Luca had an amazing talent for cooking vegan and we were the beneficiaries of that talent. Had I been too busy to notice; had my reporting systems and procedures not been put in place to note his disengagement; had I been too set in my ways and uncaring to acknowledge another point of view, I would have performance managed him out of his role, and out the door. By taking the time to understand what Luca was passionate about, I found a way to help him profit from his passions and tap into his natural talents, and in the process, make a profit for my business and our investors. Everyone's a winner.

Luca's been one of my most loyal staff members and that's due to the fact I let him explore his passions under my roof so he could unleash his inner entrepreneur.

HOW TO BENEFIT FROM YOUR TEAM'S PERSONAL PASSIONS

Gina was the head bar attendant at one of our pubs. She was a fashionista who always rocked up to work in something loud and outrageous and kept the patrons entertained with stories from her time working in New York's hottest bars. Turns out, she's an extraordinary graphic designer too and was working at the pub part time to pay her way through a fine arts degree. When we sat down for our 'meal' to check how she was going and get some insights into what I could do to nurture her intrapreneurial talents, she told me what she was studying, so I said, 'Could you bring your artistic talent to the pub?' She grabbed her bag, fired up her iPad and showed me a web page filled with some stunning bar menu designs she had created at her last job. 'These are my designs. If you'd like something like that for here, I could do it for you too. I have to create a portfolio for my university course. I may as well use the pub as my guinea pig'.

I didn't need convincing.

I gave her the nod to commence, and within a few weeks, we had a completely reimagined drinks list, coupled with a high-end cocktail printed menu, and a spectacular chalk board featuring hand-drawn calligraphy to showcase the menu, all created and designed by Gina. She even trained the staff on how to make the cocktails.

It never ceases to amaze me what people are capable of if they are given the opportunity to do what they love. With enough input and interest, you too could find a way to profit from your people's passions.

When ability doesn't match ambition

We've all been there. Placed a staff member in the wrong role and lived to regret it. I did it not that long ago. A valued team member, Callum, had designs on being in a senior management role. He had worked for me for two years, was a good team player and had expressed interest in taking on new responsibilities. I'm always keen to elevate ambitious staff, so when a role as Chief Experience Officer came up in one of my pubs, I gave him the role. I paid for him and his family to be transferred to the new location, set them up in a house and he got to work. His job was to train new staff, introduce new products into the venues, work with the licensees to show them how to implement the new products and inspire the customers to try those new products.

Within a few weeks, cracks appeared in the surface: he didn't respond to emails quickly, he'd bring his kids into the office (and they'd stay there all day), basic reporting didn't get done and he became stressed and struggled to manage the demands of the role. I found this out through a combination of sources: other staff, customers and our performance appraisal (a series of conversations and a survey), which is thankfully very robust, and from that a fairly well-rounded view emerged. The upshot? Callum was not up to the task. He was attracted to the thought of the role, but he just didn't have the knowledge or skill to do it.

I take responsibility for Callum not working out. The irony was he was hired to train staff on our new customer service systems and procedures, but the reality was we didn't provide him with the training he needed to do it. We moved him into the role too quickly, and while we surrounded him with the tools needed to do the work, he didn't have the training or competencies to use those tools.

We moved Callum back to one of our other pubs, he returned to his old role and he was happy. He tried, we tried, but the experiment didn't work out.

What we did do well was act quickly. Once we realised it wasn't working out, we took immediate action to ensure the situation was resolved so that further collateral damage to the pub, the profitability and the brand was minimised.

Be slow to criticise and quick to praise

If you aren't happy with a staff member, a supplier or any other stakeholder, don't wait until you're about to sack them or move them on to tell them. Give them short, sharp feedback as quickly as possible and watch to see if the behaviour improves. If it doesn't, you've got your answer, but at least you gave them the chance to correct their ways.

I had an accountancy firm that had been doing great work for me, but as their business grew, the service we received diminished. I gave them feedback and was quite clear about what was lacking but after a few weeks, the service remained unchanged. They were expensive and generally good at what they did, but the time had come to find a new supplier who would give us the rolled gold standard we were paying for and deserved, so I decided to move on and choose a new firm to work with. Interestingly, our new provider not only dedicated a team to our business but was also cheaper than the old one. I've learned over the years that price is not always indicative of quality, so don't get swayed into believing that more expensive equals better.

Similarly, if someone is doing a great job, tell them quickly and often. I recall working for a large club operator. I felt like I wasn't making an impact or getting advanced as quickly as I had hoped. When I was head-hunted for a new role, I took it, gave notice and asked for a reference. My boss agreed to write one, and it was glowing! I had no idea he held me in such high esteem. If I had known what he really thought of me, I might not have left.

Reinvesting in your team

Just as properties need to be maintained and updated, so too do your people. We work hard to keep our staff happy and loyal. Here's how we do it.

Top 6 ways to build staff morale / a top team

1. Always praise in public and punish in private.

2. Involve them in the decision-making process.

3. Communicate with them regularly.

4. Forgive if they have made an honest mistake.

5. Get rid of dead wood.

6. Get rid of dead wood quickly.

Training

We invest heavily in staff training. I have suffered the consequences of promoting staff beyond their capability and when their ability doesn't match their ambition, they will inevitably fail, which means they lose, I lose, the business suffers and we lose valuable time, money and energy.

Mentoring

Our performance appraisal process quickly identifies up-and-coming superstars. They are given the opportunity to be paired with a general manager who mentors them, shows them the ropes and provides them with a structured learning plan. They also have access to advice and counselling through our employee assistance program.

Staff reward days

Our staff love this perk of working for us. We're in hospitality so it makes sense we reward our team by taking them out to enjoy a dinner and a show. While we're enjoying it all, they're also seeing other operators in action, noting what's working, what's not and experiencing first-hand what awesome (or awful) food and service looks like.

I took my team to a famous hotelier's new venue. It was lauded as being the hottest, hippest venue in town. It might have been, but someone should have informed the staff of that because they didn't look like they were enjoying themselves one little bit. They didn't smile, were short and sharp with their responses and we had to wave our hand in the air to get their attention.

Later that night, I did a debrief with the team. Having seen what we saw, I didn't need to tell the team the importance of a smile, eye contact and a warm demeanour. They had seen and felt the absence of it and the impact it had on their overall experience of the night out. No amount of training in a classroom can convey that learning. Instead of telling them what to do or how to be, I ask them to watch others in action and that experience becomes a visceral moment that they remember long after the event has taken place. This is the fastest way to train a team.

Team-building events

Other events I take my team to include major sporting events like the Newcastle Knights rugby league matches as well as cricket test matches and horse racing days. These occasions lend themselves very nicely to the staff having a few drinks and letting their hair down, all of which is great for team bonding, shared experiences and storytelling.

When staff know about each other's lives outside of work, and are cognisant of any pressures, illnesses or situations that may adversely affect someone's ability to do their work, they are far more likely to be helpful, compassionate and tolerant of that person, rather than judgemental and critical. You know the phrase: a team that plays together, stays together.

HOW TO COLLABORATE WITH SUPPLIERS TO GET THE BEST FROM YOUR TEAM

You might be thinking: *Well it's all right for him to take his staff to fancy schmancy dinner joints. But what about me? I don't have two brass razoos to rub together and the most I can afford for my team is a Domino's pizza. What can I do to reward staff?*

There are lots of ways to reward and incentivise people if you're on a budget and money is tight. For example, you could set an internal team challenge where they have to achieve a certain goal, and you create teams to foster a sense of healthy competition. You can also involve your suppliers, who will mostly jump at the chance to be a part of your competition because it means more exposure for them — and more sales.

One fun and efficient way we train our staff is we buddy them up with our suppliers so we can share the costs and the benefits of having an upskilled team. For example, we buddy with a local brewery called Grainfed. Lachie, the head brewer, invites our staff in to his brewery, the team get to try different beers, are shown how the beers get brewed, are taken on a tour of the production line to see how it all works and are trained in understanding the various processes used to create different beers.

There are literally hundreds of different beers on the market now — from craft and lagers to porters and full strength — and the staff can't possibly

(continued)

be across them all without some form of training. The benefits are obvious. Lachie gets to showcase his product to my team so they can be better skilled at selling it. We benefit because our team can answer any questions from customers about the beer. This makes us look good and makes the customer buy more beer. Everyone wins.

Summing up ...

1. The three most important elements in a business are people, people, people.

2. Having a meal with a prospective team member may reveal more about them than a formal interview process.

3. Don't make assumptions without getting all the facts. Listen, observe, ask questions, take notes and then respond.

4. Check the references of everyone you employ.

5. If you want to keep staff loyal, use an Employee Stock Options Program (ESOP) to share some of your success with them.

6. Unlock your team's intrapreneurial energy by helping them find work they love to do within your organisation.

7. If you elevate staff to a new role or position, ensure they get the training they need to succeed in the role.

8. Praise in public. Criticise in private.

9. Your team is a capital investment. Reinvest in them in the same way you'd reinvest in an investment property.

10. Collaborate with your suppliers to enlist them in helping you train your team.

CHAPTER 7
Build your resilience

> There is no such thing as pure pleasure; some anxiety always goes with it.
>
> *Ovid*

At some point in your business journey, you'll need to have conversations you don't want to have. 'Speaking the unspoken' is what I call it. These unpleasant little chats are also called 'tough conversations'. They're just part and parcel of being a business owner. Whether you're leading a two-person operation or a team of hundreds, a time will come when you need to hold people to account.

I had to have a tough conversation with Terry, a trusted staff member of 15 years' standing, about the theft of a significant amount of money. He had not been discreet in the way he took the money so it was easy to detect, and our systems were so robust that it didn't take long for the anomaly to show up. He was probably wanting to be found out. Sarah, one of my administrative team staff, noticed the money being moved around and told me. That, in itself, was a brave move on Sarah's part, as she knew

Terry was a long-standing member of my team and that it would be a tough conversation for her to have with me.

I dreaded having the conversation with Terry, but it needed to be had urgently. As always, I prepared extensively for the meeting using—ironically, considering the subject matter—my LOAN process. I called him in, sat him down, told him what we had suspected and then gave him time to explain himself. I listened, observed, asked questions, made notes and, having given him the time to present his position, was able to provide him with a plan going forward. It was difficult because he denied having taken the money, but the paper trail was there for everyone to see. It was clear he could no longer work with us, and we assisted him with getting psychological help and provided him with a 'fair leave' to exit the business. The process was unemotional, direct and based on facts, which enabled the unspoken to be spoken.

Tough conversations like this are never easy, but if you approach them in a clear and unemotional way, with the facts documented and bullet pointed and the supporting documentation in place, they can be done efficiently and swiftly.

He eventually paid the money back and I let bygones be bygones. We still catch up for a beer occasionally. I won't be lending him the keys to my car or my house any time soon, but everyone makes mistakes and deserves to be forgiven. I learned three important lessons from this situation: always speak the unspoken, empower your team to speak up when they see bad behaviour and implement good systems so you can spot inconsistencies quickly.

How to manage bad days

There are some days when I know I'm a little bit flat, down or intemperate. It happens to everyone and with my ADHD, it can really flare up if I'm not careful and put me in an unresourceful frame of mind. On days like that, I say I'm 'a little bit off' in that I'm not in a position to do or make important decisions, have tough conversations or review detailed documents.

Sometimes, of course, I can't avoid that so I have found strategies that really help me get back into the zone. They sound simple, and they are, but many of us overlook the banal in favour of the exotic and overcomplicate it. In short, if you're feeling 'off', it could be because you're over tired, over hungry or over thirsty. If you're any of those, take action to get some rest, some food or a drink. It'll make all the difference. Holding a tough conversation is difficult in itself. Don't go into stressful meetings without ensuring you are in tip-top mental condition, and don't make it worse by bringing less than your best self to the table.

No mud, no lotus

In 2015, I took my family on a road trip to Darwin. Our first port of call was the Adelaide River to see the world-famous saltwater crocodiles. As we made our way down the wooden jetty, we were greeted by our tour guide, 'Crocodile Pat', a crusty old fisherman with a finger missing from each hand, which, he later revealed, were sitting in the belly of Big Beryl, the largest and oldest crocodile in the river. Unfortunately, Big Beryl didn't show herself that day, but we did see the most extraordinarily beautiful display of voluptuous white flowers emanating out of the muddy mangroves. There were thousands of them, each one untouched and utterly perfect.

'What are those flowers?' I asked Crocodile Pat.

'Lotus,' he said, clearly a man of few words.

'How does a beautiful flower like that grow here?' my wife asked.

'It loves the mud,' he said.

What a paradox.

I did some 'digging' around to discover more about the lotus and found out how and why it can thrive in such a hostile and unwelcoming environment. Turns out, its roots are deeply latched into the mud and it derives all its minerals and nutrients from the mud in which it sits.

More research showed that the lotus is a special flower and is considered to be one of the most sacred plants in the world, particularly the Buddhist world. I can see why. For a start, it has a lifecycle unlike any other plant. Every night, it sinks beneath the murky water, absorbs the nutrients it needs and then emerges at sunrise the next day, sparkling clean and ready to face the day. Not only does it find sanctuary in the mud and muck, but the waxy film on its petals protects it from getting dirtied by the mud.

If there's a better metaphor for life and business, I'm yet to find it. In other words: no mud, no lotus.

Kim Kardashian and *that* sex tape

There are countless stories of entrepreneurs' careers that began in the mud and rose to become the lotus. Kim Kardashian's empire is one.

It's a much-forgotten fact that the Kardashian empire was kickstarted by a lurid sex tape. Kim's 'boyfriend' at the time, R&B singer Ray J, filmed them having sex and that video found its way onto the internet. At the time, Kim was mostly famous for being Paris Hilton's personal assistant and the daughter of Robert Kardashian, the infamous lawyer who defended OJ Simpson. But the video changed all that. Enough with the backstory.

After the video went to air, the internet went nuts, Kim became famous for all the wrong reasons and the rest is history. (And before you say 'who cares about the Kardashians', a recent tweet by Kylie Jenner (Kim's half-sister) saw the share price of Snapchat plummet by 6 per cent in one day! These gals have clout.)

The point is, without that sex tape, the world may have been deprived of Kim Kardashian and we may never have seen the likes of her or her sisters. That tape was the mud. Her career (all $1 billion of it) is the lotus. You don't have to look too far to find more stories where entrepreneurs have found themselves waist deep in mud and used that experience to rise to the top, sparkling clean, just like the lotus.

My mud, my lotus

My minor version of the mud/lotus story has nothing to do with sex tapes. (Sorry. Your loss.) But it has everything to do with the Catholic church. This is getting weird. Stay with me.

Some of the most positive and exciting opportunities in my business career have come about when I've been deep in the mud: moments when I wasn't sure how I was going to get out of it.

Here's one that is forever etched in my mind.

In 2003, I was gearing up for a big St Stephen's celebration at The Kent pub. It's one of my favourite days of the year, not for the obvious reason that we share the same name, but because it's one of the most lucrative days of the year for our pub. People are out and about: on holiday, ready to party and more importantly, ready to spend.

In case you're wondering, St Stephen's Day is also known as Boxing Day. It was created to honour one of the first Christian martyrs, St Stephen, who was stoned to death in 36 CE. Harsh. It's called Boxing Day because it was a day when the rich delivered a 'boxed'-up present for their servants in recognition of their service.

Fortunately for us, our pub happens to be near a major horse-racing track. The Boxing Day races at Broadmeadow attract more than 20 000 people, most of whom end up in our pub after the last race. People, punting, pints, parties: you can see why it's my favourite day of the year.

We were expecting a massive day so I rostered seven of my best security guards on for the day, and I planned to station them at all the doors (and windows — you'd be amazed at the lengths people go to beat the queues) to ensure no unsavoury sorts would descend and ruin this most fabulous day. We knew the races finished at 5 pm so we were fully prepared for anything and everything that the day held in store ... except for the rain, which came belting down at 2 pm. We weren't prepared for that because it was the height of summer and normally stinking hot. Instead of people fleeing for home, they flocked to our pub three hours ahead of schedule, and crucially, two hours before my security guards were ready to start work. We were totally unprepared to manage that volume of guests at that time of the day.

As luck would have it, this was the very day the liquor licensing squad decided to inspect our pub. We knew they'd be paying us a visit at some time, but we didn't realise they'd be doing it at 2 pm, the exact moment when thousands of people fleeing the rain were flooding through our doors, with not enough security guards to monitor and manage the crowd.

People were everywhere. They were lined up at the door, crawling through the windows, climbing up the balcony, sneaking through the kitchen. *Everywhere*. In normal circumstances, I would have been rubbing my hands with glee at this level of patronage. But that day, I was wringing them with worry. What had been so meticulously planned was fast becoming a nightmare. This one event could see my business shut down virtually overnight. We were in the mud and there was not a lotus in sight.

I quickly gathered my team and said, 'We need to buy some time. What can we do?' One of them said, 'How about we charge them a cover fee to get in?'

'How will that help?' I asked.

'It will deter some from coming in, slow down the rest and buy us time until our security guys turn up.'

'Genius,' I said. 'Let's do it.'

We hastily sourced a trestle table from the basement, found an ink stamp and a cash tin, and proceeded to charge every guest $5 for the privilege of coming through our doors. We had never charged people to enter our pubs before and were slightly worried we'd cop some flak from the regulars, but they could see we were getting hammered and were happy to pay just to get into what was fast becoming the biggest party of the year.

The impact of this hastily conceived but incredibly powerful strategy was immediate.

It slowed down the flow of people entering until our security guards turned up. It helped us monitor the crowd and gave us the opportunity to pick and choose who we let in (because, as you know, once you let them in, it's very difficult to get them out) and most importantly, it prevented the police from shutting us down. (And we made $5000 in the process. A handy little win.)

Now, whenever we have a big event planned, especially in this COVID-19 environment where we can't anticipate who will turn up or when, we have a simple strategy we can employ to manage the crowds and keep the police and the other authorities happy. This experience was transformative for me and my team. We prevailed at a time of extreme stress and found a creative (and profitable) way to get through a very difficult set of circumstances.

Since then, whenever I find myself 'stuck in the mud', facing an uphill battle or struggling to see a solution, I repeat to myself, 'no mud, no lotus', and know that a solution is nearby. I take great comfort in knowing that sometimes when you are in the deepest mud, the most unexpected opportunities will, like the lotus, arise and blossom.

THERE'S ALWAYS A POSITIVE, IF YOU LOOK FOR IT

In my constant endeavour to improve myself and to step out of my comfort zone, I decided to apply to speak at my industry's most prestigious event, the Las Vegas Nightclub and Bar Show. It's the world's largest bar and nightclub trade convention and anyone and everyone in the hotel or hospitality sector attends. I had been a few years previously and seen the calibre of speakers on the agenda so I knew it would be a great opportunity. To my delight, they said 'Yes!' I was stoked but shitting myself at the same time.

I prepared my speech, rehearsed it like crazy, felt the nerves, questioned why I was putting myself through all this, contemplated cancelling it all, got excited again, kept rehearsing and just tried to keep my head in the

(continued)

game as to why I was doing this as I knew the rewards of public speaking would far outweigh the costs.

And then COVID-19 came along! The show was cancelled and all bets were off. I was devastated. I'd spent months working on my speech, but as I always say to myself, 'no mud, no lotus'. I looked at the speech I had written and thought, 'This would make a good book', so I turned the speech into a book (the one you're reading right now).

If the conference hadn't been cancelled, I may never have written this book. The conference will be on again and I've got a standing invitation to speak at it so maybe the cancellation was a blessing in disguise.

Don't annoy the authorities

You may not know this, but we publicans are duty bound by the liquor laws to stop people from getting drunk in our establishments. We support these laws. Yes, we like people to drink—it's an important part of our business—but we certainly don't benefit at all when people are heavily intoxicated. Fights, injuries, ambulances, police, sirens, dogs: these are not generally considered good for anyone's business, let alone a house of fun, which is what a pub is.

So, when these liquor laws were enacted, we needed to find a way to work with the police to ensure we were able to comply in a fair and reasonable way. But before we had the chance to do that, we found ourselves in a situation that caused us a great deal of reputational damage, cost us upwards of $250 00 in legal fees and could have struck us off as directors or licensees of a hotel for 10 years.

It all started when a rather industrious policeman issued us with a low-level infringement for inconsequential issues. When doing our daily signage audits, we missed putting a sign over the door that read, 'Minors must be accompanied by an adult at all times'. The fine, which was issued without a warning, was $2000. In the scheme of things, it was a pretty small fine, but the fact was, we knew we had followed the rule of law and had taken all reasonable steps to comply with the directions, and yet they still issued the fine.

I knew that contesting the fine would be time consuming and expensive, but I also thought, *If I don't stand up for my team, and protect them from this unjust fine, what kind of leader am I?* A pretty piss poor one, I would think.

So, I decided to fight it, and that's when all the 'fun and games' started.

We fronted up to court, defended ourselves and won. It was a waste of time and money for everyone, but the police were keen to make an example of a random pub owner to demonstrate their might. It was a victory for sense over nonsense but the police didn't take kindly to losing the case.

So, when this next brouhaha occurred—a much, much more serious situation than we had ever faced before—we found our options of resolving it with the assistance of the police severely hampered. After all, if the police are against you, who do you turn to for help?

Here's what happened.

TAKING ON THE AUTHORITIES

It was a Saturday night at my busiest pub, The Kent. How busy? One thousand people per night busy. That's a lot of people. As a result, you do what you need to and hire security guards. I'm a big believer that the best way to stop bad people from being in my venue is to prevent them from getting into it in the first place. As a result, security guards are a critical element in ensuring my pubs operate seamlessly and with as few headaches as possible.

What I didn't know was that one of my security guards (let's call him Nigel), a man who'd been with me for three years, was on duty that night and was selling ecstasy tablets to my patrons (and had been doing so for months).

(continued)

So, when a staff member came to me and said, 'Steve, I think we have a problem. I have it on good authority that Nigel is selling drugs to our patrons, and he's doing it on your premises, on your time,' my blood ran cold.

Nigel wasn't acting alone here either. He wasn't some dead-beat, two-bit, small-time junkie looking to score a few bucks to pay for his next hit. No. Nigel was part of an elaborate drug cartel that was responsible for supplying the vast bulk of illegal drugs to the partygoers of Newcastle and surrounds. He was a pro.

We called Nigel into the office and sacked him on the spot based on our suspicions. He kicked up a stink saying he had been unfairly dismissed, tossed a few chairs around, and stormed out.

After he left, it became apparent there was something else I didn't know. For the past three months, a major drug operation featuring a parade of undercover detectives had been frequenting my pub, acting as patrons and buying drugs from Nigel! What I did know, however, was that if the police had caught Nigel dealing drugs on my premises, there was a chance I could also be arrested for being an accessory and an accomplice for encouraging this kind of criminal activity.

This is called 'entrapment' and while it's illegal in many places, it's not in New South Wales. So, when a trio of undercover detectives decided to lay in wait to entrap Nigel, there was not much I could do.

To even contemplate that we would risk our business to sell drugs on the dancefloor beggars belief. But try telling that to these undercover detectives, determined to make us pay for beating them in court a year earlier. This was serious. Deadly serious.

I was innocent of the charges levelled against me, but the police were determined to make an example of me.

To make matters worse, the police went public with the drug bust. They contacted all the media organisations, encouraged them to set up their TV cameras for a press conference and proceeded to tell the world that our pub was a 'haven for drug dealers'. We were shocked to find ourselves on the 6 pm Channel Nine news that night. The local community — people we had worked with and served for decades — turned against us and would spit on the pub window as they walked past. It was horrendous.

The injustice of it was emotionally crippling. But wallowing in this negative thinking about how I had become an unwitting pawn in a political charade wasn't going to get me out of the shit storm I was in. I had to get on with it. I had to defend myself. This was a major decision for me and my family to make. Going up against the New South Wales police (again) is not something you do lightly. I had been there before and didn't like it. But this was going to require another level of commitment, confidence and, it has to be said, cash, because running a court case isn't cheap. But I was innocent and there was no way I was ever going to back down on this.

Fast forward 13 months, and there I am in the dock in the Supreme Court in Sydney, my suite of barristers at a hefty cost of $30000 a day working their arses off. I had to take the stand at the Supreme Court three times. And it wasn't just me taking the stand. Many of my staff also had to get up and defend themselves at great cost to them, both emotionally and physically. My staff performed brilliantly under pressure, and have continued to work for me for many years after this very distressing event.

The outcome? We won. Why? One, because we were innocent, and two, because we were fortunate to be fighting the case in this great country of Australia, where, despite the fact the entrapment laws in New South Wales are harsh (and we should never have been fighting the charges in the first place), our right to the presumption of innocence sits at the heart of the Australian justice system, and it was this presumption of innocence that forced the police to justify their case.

My dad deserves a shoutout here too. His days of working at the Australian Tax Office meant he knew how the machinations of government worked. His advice was instrumental in helping us win and I'll be forever grateful to him for his support.

Could I have pleaded guilty and avoided all the headache? Absolutely. In some respects, if I didn't care about honesty and my reputation, it would have been easier to lie down and say 'do your worst'. But I do care about

(continued)

all those things, so to have them taken away by a swag of corrupt coppers who were simply out to make a point, well, that wasn't going to happen on my watch.

Fortunately, I had the funds to fight the case. But what if I didn't? What if I was a novice business owner on minimum wage and had zero access to high-paid legal advice? What then? Would I have given in? Possibly. You can't go back in time, so we'll never know, but one thing I do know is this: I am eternally grateful that we live in a country governed by the rule of law and that everyone is entitled to the presumption of innocence.

What this experience taught me

What would I do differently? Not much. If the authorities are out to get you, there's not much you can do. But what I would do (and do now) is this: I work very hard to stay ahead of the regulations and keep the authorities in the loop so that we have an open and honest relationship that can withstand the slings and arrows of the argy bargy of doing business.

Supporting your team in a crisis

They say that the art of being wise is the art of knowing what to overlook. As a publican, knowing what battles to fight and what to leave alone is a herculean task I wrestle with daily. Pubs are dynamic places and a lot can go wrong without it being anyone's direct, or specific, fault so I'm often called upon to make a judgement decision as to what we should do next when difficult situations arise.

The decisions I make can have long-range impacts on me, my family, my investors, my staff and my finances so they need to be thought through carefully. But sometimes you have to stand up for what's right and fight the battles, knowing that in the process you might lose the war. Sometimes it's not just a principle that needs defending, but my staff. They need to know I have their back and I will defend them. If I don't, it erodes trust, respect and rapport and once you've lost that, you've lost everything.

One case where I had to make a careful decision as to what battle to fight involved a staff member, Charlie, who didn't have his Responsible Serving of Alcohol (RSA) card in his wallet when he turned up for work. As (bad) luck would have it, a liquor licensing inspector decided to pay us a visit that day and requested Charlie produce his card. When he couldn't, the inspector issued us with a fine. Charlie had a copy of the RSA card on file, and was able to produce a hard copy of it for the inspector so we could prove we were abiding by the law, but because he didn't have it on his person at the time of inspection, the inspector gave us a $1200 fine.

I had two options. I could cop it sweet and pay the fine, or I could take it to court and take a chance on the judge having the common sense to see that this kind of administrivia and ridiculous red tape was not only small minded and petty, but expensive to the courts and the state in general. We chose the latter option.

Unfortunately, the judge sided with the liquor licensing inspector and fined us. Tellingly, they let us off on a 'Section 10', which meant we had to pay the fine but received no conviction. (I should add that the other two gentlemen facing court that day prior to us—a son convicted of assaulting his father, and a serious drink-driving offender—were both let off with no fine or conviction.)

I don't regret my decision to fight this case in court. Yes, Charlie should have had the card on his person that day, but who hasn't stuffed up and left a wallet at home before, or made an administrative error that in real terms didn't hurt or affect anyone? I went to court for two reasons. One, to demonstrate to my team that if they are caught in the cross fires of the authorities, and they have done the right thing in principle, I will go to great lengths to show them that I am 100 per cent behind them; that I will invest time, energy and funds to defend them in court; and that I will personally front up and speak up on their behalf. After all, if you have faith in your team, you will support them.

The second reason I went to court was because I wanted to show the judge how petty his demeanour was, and to give him the evidence he needed to change the law so that no other publican would have to go through this charade and waste valuable time and money.

Ironically, in between getting the fine and going to court, the legislation in this state changed, which means that a staff member no longer has to keep their RSA card on their person. Even with that knowledge to hand, the judge decided to fine us for the so-called offence.

Top 8 ways to support your staff and keep them loyal

1. Be honest.

2. Let them know mistakes are accepted but not expected regularly.

3. Be compassionate when they are in need.

4. Don't expect any favours.

5. Don't ask them to do anything you wouldn't do.

6. Involve them in your plans.

7. Recognise you have two ears and one mouth and they should be used in that proportion.

8. Always have boundaries and let them know what's expected.

How any small-business owner can fight for what's right

I often get asked, 'It's okay for you, Stephen, to stand up for your staff and protect them and fight these cases because you have the funds to do so. What about the little guys, the smaller operators who get shafted by the authorities but who don't have the funds to fight them. What can they do?'

Yes, I do have the funds to fight, but even when I didn't, in the early days, I always fought the battle no matter what. I once got a loan to fight a court case because I felt so strongly about what went on. Call me crazy, but I just can't sit by while bad behaviour plays out in front of me.

If you have to fight a court case for something that's unjust or unfair, and you don't have the funds, join your local association (in my case, it's the Australian Hotels Association) and lobby them to fight it with you or on your behalf. That's part of their advocacy role.

If you don't respect the lobby or advocacy group that represents your industry, get on the board yourself and change it from the inside. If you don't like what they're doing, rally your mates in the industry to step up too, so you have some voting power. Yes, I know that means 'getting involved' but if you want to enable change and solve the problem, you need to be a part of the solution. If you don't want to do that, stop whingeing because if you're not prepared to put some time and effort into helping make your industry group stronger and more powerful for the benefit of you and everyone else, why would others?

And just remember this: irrespective of how big your business is or how many people you employ, your voice can make an impact. Everyone has the power to make a difference.

Summing up...

1. Don't be afraid to have the tough conversations and to speak the unspoken with everyone in your team.

2. Forgive people if they make a mistake, and don't hold grudges. Everyone is human.

3. Support your team in a crisis. They need to know you have their back.

4. If you don't have the financial capacity to fight a legal battle, seek help from your industry association.

CHAPTER 8
Build your knowledge

While most people come to pubs to have fun, some have other intentions, and this potential for violence to erupt at any time needs to be carefully managed. Knowledge is power and forewarned is forearmed, so we work hard to ensure everyone is safe. Most customers wouldn't see the seedier side of things (and we try really hard to protect them from seeing it) but when you get alcohol, late nights, high emotion and large numbers of people in close proximity (some possibly with illegal substances coursing through their systems), you get trouble.

You never know who you're dealing with

Having managed and owned pubs all my adult life, I've seen the shabbier side of things a lot and I've had to develop strategies and systems for managing the violence when it erupts. Knowing who you're dealing with is part of that.

Growing up, my old man was pretty strict, but he taught me how to stand up for myself. This quality has set me in good stead because I now have zero tolerance for bad or disrespectful behaviour towards anyone. Call me stupid, misguided or naïve, but when I see anyone—women, kids, men—mistreated or mishandled, verbally or physically, I need to step in. Has it cost me? You bet. Have I got involved in situations that I shouldn't have? You bet. But I can't stand bullies and will step up to stamp out bullying when I see it. It takes me back to my childhood when I was bullied and I couldn't do much to confront it. Now I can, and I do.

One time when I felt I had to take action is seared in my mind. I was working at a great little pub in the middle of London. My boss, Frank, would often give out fliers to promote discounted drinks at a late-night club just down the road, so after work we'd all head down there to catch up with mates and snare a few free drinks. It was a seedy little joint, but full of atmosphere. The entrance was down a dark stairway, the walls were lined with photographs of famous rock bands and it smelled musty and dank from decades of spilt beer. It was fantastic. On this night, the place was packed with people, the drinks were flowing, the music was pumping—it was going off.

We had settled in at the bar to listen to the band when, out of the corner of my eye, I saw this big, beefy guy get up and king hit the guy standing next to me. This innocent man had not provoked him or done anything to warrant that violence. He lay on the floor, moaning in agony, and then this oaf and three of his mates started kicking the guy in the stomach and stomping on his head. I stood up to drag them off, which made them turn on me. My two mates saw what was happening, jumped in to help me and, within seconds, there was a massive pile-on in the middle of this tiny club. These four thugs, all dressed in identical football guernseys, grabbed their schooner glasses, smashed them on the edge of the bar and tried to stab us, and everyone nearby, with the shards. It was deadset insane behaviour.

The security guards, illegal immigrants from South Africa, bolted up the stairs and out the door, unwilling to get caught in the affray for fear of being deported. That left us (and the other customers who were being hammered) to fend for ourselves against these drug-fuelled idiots.

We eventually bear-wrestled them all up the stairs, threw them out and locked the doors. Within seconds, we heard an almighty crash as a window to my left exploded. As the glass literally rained down on me, I saw a foot crash through the broken window, quickly followed by a leg, an arm and then a torso of the same guy we had just chucked out. His arms were red raw and bleeding, and then his head appeared at the window, screaming all manner of obscenities. He reminded me of Jack Nicholson in *The Shining*. I punched him in the face, but that didn't stop him. He got in and reached over to open the door to let his mates in, but we held him back.

Next thing we knew, there was another leg, arm, torso and bloodied head coming in through another broken window. This guy's face was cut up from the glass and bleeding too, but that didn't stop him from throwing punches. If you've ever seen the film *World War Z* with Brad Pitt, you'll know what I mean when I say these guys were like crazed zombies committed to their cause, which was to get back into the pub, no matter what. We called the police and shouted at the hooligans, 'The cops are coming!' but that didn't deter them at all.

'We don't give a fuck!' they said. 'Don't you know who we are?'

I didn't, and I told them so, but nothing was going to stop them. Eventually, the police came, but by that time the thugs had moved on.

I went back the next day to check in with my mates and debrief what had happened. They weren't there, but the manager—an ex-cop who hadn't been on duty that night—was, and he invited me for a coffee. He'd heard all about it. He looked at my cut hands and bruised face and said, 'Are you okay?'

'Yeah, but a bit shaken.'

'Thank you for doing what you did. This could have been a whole lot worse if you and your friends hadn't stepped in. Do you know who those thugs were? Did you recognise any of them?'

'I've never seen them before,' I said. 'But they were all wearing the same kind of shirt. A red football guernsey with the word "Fulham" on it.'

He went white.

'What?' I said, worried that he was worried.

'That's the Fulham Gang.'

'Who are they?'

'Only the most notorious soccer hooligans in England. They're drug-fuelled maniacs who wouldn't hesitate to slit your throat if you so much as looked sideways at them. I can't believe you took them on. Even the cops are scared of them.'

'Well I'm not, but I'm glad I didn't know who they were before I started throwing them out.'

'Let's hope they don't remember you.'

Maybe I should have googled 'Fulham' before I got into that fight, but hey, Google wasn't around then. If I had, I might have used some different techniques to diffuse the tension, like hightailing it out of there alongside the South African security guards. Bottom line: you need to know who you're dealing with in business.

I was pretty confrontational as a young man, but I've since learned that you catch more bees with honey than you do with vinegar. I've also learned to defuse tension using more sophisticated techniques than my previous tactics. Here are a few of them.

Top 10 ways to defuse conflict or aggression

1. Always remain calm.

2. Divide and conquer.

3. Remove any objects that could be used as a weapon.

4. Always have your hands raised in a calm manner.

5. Try to assess why they are upset.

6. See if you can talk to them in a quiet place.

7. Don't crowd them into a corner.

8. Don't raise your voice.

9. Sometimes it's best to have a member of the opposite sex talk to them (women can be better at calming down an angry man).

10. Try to guide them close to a door.

What it says 'on the box' is not necessarily what's 'in the box'

Have you seen those internet memes about fast-food restaurants comparing and contrasting what's advertised on the outside of the box with what you actually get inside the box? For example, on the left of the page, it shows the picture of a luscious juicy burger with a slice of rich red tomato, a slab of melting cheese oozing down the side and a flourish of crisp green lettuce, all smothered in a flowing chipotle sauce. It looks delicious. On the right-hand side, it shows the picture of what you actually get: a flaccid, wet bun sliding around in a gelatinous green and red sauce.

Just as you need to know who you're dealing with in business, you need to do your due diligence about what you're buying. Before you buy a business, take out a lease, hire staff or buy stock, you really need to have a good, hard look at what you're really getting because when people sell a business, what's 'on the box' isn't necessarily what's 'in the box'.

To avoid getting ripped off, you must do your due diligence. It may sound boring but it's not when you consider what it will cost you if you don't. Many business owners fail to do the most basic research, and that failure to delve into the detail comes back to haunt them.

THE COST OF NOT DOING YOUR DUE DILIGENCE

Paul is a local fitness gym owner. He took out a lease on a fitness studio, spent $50 000 on a fit-out, invested $20 000 to advertise his new business, held his open day and had dozens of new clients sign up. It was all going so brilliantly. But the day after launch, he opened his local newspaper to discover that the strip of road his business was on was being bought back by the council to make way for a massive highway extension. He rang the council to clarify the situation and was told that within 12 months he would need to be out of the property. He was gobsmacked that the authorities hadn't notified him. He was also taken aback that his real estate agent would offer him a lease knowing the construction was about to take place. When he rang the agent to complain, he said, 'Not my problem', which was code for, 'You should have done your homework'.

Paul was devastated to learn that he would have to leave the premises, find a new property, pay to have it fitted out (again) and lose a stack of customers along the way. Personally, I felt for the bloke as he invested his life savings in this endeavour, but at the same time, I did think he was naïve in taking out a lease without doing the bare minimum of due diligence.

Could Paul have done some research about upcoming road developments? Could he have scheduled meetings with the council to give him a heads-up on what was being planned? Yes, and yes. Most of this information would have been in the public domain somewhere and even a hint of what was to come may have indicated that the location was going to be more of a headache than what it was worth. If he'd hired a lawyer to review the leasing documents, they would no doubt have unearthed the council plans and advised him not to proceed.

What's certain is that Paul will do his due diligence next time to ensure he is not blind-sided by council or local government developments.

Sometimes we have to be hit hard financially to learn a valuable lesson.

What does 'doing due diligence' actually mean?

Given that I was an energetic, undiagnosed ADHD kid, my parents were forever telling me to 'sit still', 'pay attention' and 'do your homework!' If only they could see me, they'd be so pleased to know that I now excel at doing my homework. I just call it something else—due diligence—and whether you're studying for school exams or buying a business, you need to do it.

If you're buying a business, or investing in one, it means asking for information about that business so you can make an informed decision on whether you'll buy or invest in it. Most experienced investors won't invest in anything until they see a document called an information memorandum (or IM). It's also known as a business plan or simply 'the plan'. (What you call it will be influenced by how you structure your company and what you're purporting to offer.)

An IM is a document produced by the seller that tells you 'what's in the box'. It contains proprietary information about the business, such as sales, expenses, assets, trademarks, intellectual property and so on and in general is designed to look very impressive. It's meant to, as its sole purpose is to sell the business from one party to another. The only trouble with these polished works of art is that what they say or purport to offer isn't always what you get.

It takes a trained eye to identify whether the information contained in an IM is correct or not. A good (but not necessarily ethical) accountant can work wonders with numbers and make things either magically appear or disappear. That's why you need a first-class accountant to help you review these figures and make sure everything in the IM stacks up.

What you need before buying any bricks and mortar business

When I buy a pub (or any bricks and mortar business, really), these are some of the documents I ask the seller to provide as part of my due diligence:

- a development approval from council showing the location is approved for use as a licensed premises

- a development approval from council for any alterations/ additions and signage

- details of employees (length of service, salaries, long service leave, other entitlements)

- a survey of the land

- inventory of plant and equipment to be included in the sale

- the last three years' profit-and-loss statements and the last quarter's figures.

This is the bare minimum that you would seek to obtain from the seller to ensure your due diligence has been conducted in a comprehensive manner. Ask your accountant to review these figures and contracts to ensure they are accurate, compare them with other like-for-like businesses (or any business) and make an assessment as to the veracity of the information you've been provided.

Look ahead

The due diligence phase can elicit a lot of information that could deter you from proceeding. However, on the flip side, I've seen business owners use that same due diligence to turn a negative situation into a profitable positive opportunity.

HOW TO TURN NEGATIVE NEWS INTO PROFITABLE OPPORTUNITIES

Rosemary has a very successful beauty salon in Brighton, 10 kilometres south of Melbourne. She has been operating from the premises for more than 20 years and it has grown to become the locals' 'go-to' salon for waxing, tanning and cosmetic procedures. Unlike Paul, she had her finger on the pulse of what council were planning and discovered in her due diligence that the railway crossing a few metres from her building was scheduled for removal, and a tunnel was to be built under it.

While the date for the removal of the level crossing wasn't declared, she knew it was coming and decided to take swift action. Most business owners would see this need to move premises as a negative and rue the costs and loss of trade as downsides. Not Rosemary. She saw it as an opportunity to choose a property that matched her vision, that could service a higher number of customers and that offered better car parking. A property that could position her as the premiere beauty salon in the region, enable her to charge a premium for her service and increase her profit margins.

Were there costs involved? Was it disruptive? Did she lose customers in the process while the new premises were being established? Yes, it was costly, but not nearly as costly as staying where she was, being caught short-footed and experiencing the stress of being on the wrong end of a road development and losing her entire business.

By the time construction works started, she was out of the premises, had given her customers plenty of notice, had the new 'We've moved' signage ready to go, and was able to enact a seamless transition from one place to the next.

It was interesting to observe the businesses in the same shopping strip that didn't take advance action. Like Paul, they didn't see the writing on the wall or do their own due diligence. They stayed where they were; they didn't take action to find new premises or notify their customers of the upcoming disruption. When the railway construction commenced, they watched the high-vis workers move in and the 'Road closed' signs go up.

(continued)

This disruption took away all of the foot and road traffic that they relied on for custom. Within weeks, their sales slowed to a trickle and their income along with it. Within months, the 'For lease' signs went up, accompanied by the note, 'Thank you for your custom. Regrettably, we have decided to close down due to the lack of trade'.

No-one likes to see a business fade, but those business owners who choose not to do their due diligence have to wear the consequences. Paul could have taken action 12 months earlier to ensure the closure didn't happen. Yes, it would have been a lot of work and expense but he'd still have his business.

The debacle Paul experienced represents what can happen if you don't carry out your due diligence. The success Rosemary enjoyed represents what can happen if you do carry out your due diligence.

The message is clear. If you want to make sure that 'what's on the box' is 'what's in the box', do your due diligence before outlaying any cash, time or energy. Remember: the document you must ask the seller to provide is the information memorandum. Don't move a muscle until you get it.

Waste not, want not

'Building your knowledge' extends to not just knowing how to maximise efficiencies within your business, but knowing how to maximise energy. We all know that running your own business can be exhausting. There's so much to do, and the buck stops with you. I have seven pubs, 1.4 million customers per year, 50 investors, $100 million under management, five children, a wife, sporting and charitable endeavours, community roles and much more. All of that requires energy, so if there's any opportunity to conserve, contain, harness or retain it, I do it.

Energy comes in many forms and I work hard to maximise it all so that nothing is wasted. Wastage of any sort drives me crazy. Whether it's time, labour, electricity, food or water, nothing gets under my skin more than the inefficient use of resources. I call it 'leakage' because it's like a leaky tap, and the water is your profit, going down the drain, one drop at a time.

Wastage shows up in the smallest of ways. For example, a key indicator that a pub is wasting resources is when the big screen TV in the sports bar is turned off. Clearly someone doesn't have it in their job description to turn the TV on each day. While this seems trivial, it impacts the bottom line. How? For a start, the pub had to pay for the TV, so there's a $9000 leakage right there. It's plugged into the wall so the pub has to pay for electricity whether the TV is being used or not. That's leakage. They're paying a fee to show the football games on that TV, which is also leakage because no-one gets to watch the game. The patron is paying to have an experience and without the game showing, they lose out on what they came in for, which impacts the atmosphere in the pub, which impacts who comes into the pub, which impacts what they spend in the pub, and on it goes. Leakage everywhere, multiplied day after day, month after month, simply because someone, somewhere, didn't know it was their job to turn the TV on. Systems matter.

The dining room in the Duke Hotel.

Why I hate waste

Leakage occurs with people too. That sounds a bit weird but when it comes to managing staff, the team need to know where they stand, and good reporting systems like performance reviews, informal catch-ups, dashboards and surveys help to achieve that. For example, if you have an issue with a staff member, it's best to find that out quickly, have a chat, sort it out and then make sure that behaviour doesn't show up again. Just having that conversation in itself is instructive as there may be something going on with that person you don't know about— something that's outside that person's control and isn't their fault. They then get the chance to explain what they're doing, and why, and then you can make a calculated decision about what to do next. Letting bad behaviour drag on, or finding out about it six months after it's occurred, is too late. Having systems in place like we do can pick up small problems before they become big problems.

Summing up ...

1. You never know who you're dealing with. Do your research to find out the background of those you're working with.

2. Before you buy or invest in a business, do your due diligence. It will cost far more later on if you don't.

3. Ask the seller of the business for an information memorandum so you can do your due diligence.

4. Energy comes in many guises: time, labour, electricity, food, water, money. Take care not to waste any of it.

Part III
SELL

You've found your passion, built your assets, team, culture, confidence, resilience and knowledge. You've honed your appetite for risk, implemented processes and procedures for mitigating that risk, and created fall-back positions and safeguarding systems for when stuff happens that you just can't control.

Now it's time to reap the rewards of all your hard work. It's time to bring your 'baby' to market and see what people will pay for it. Whether you sell the business completely, sell part of it (and stay on as a part owner) or seek investment from private investors, venture capitalists or equity crowdfunding, you'll need to adopt a raft of different mindsets, behaviours and procedures to make it happen. This process will require a level of commitment and focus that may take you way out of your comfort zone.

You'll be presenting and pitching to people who will want to know what you sell, who you sell it to, who your competitors are, what the growth trajectory is, what the cash position is, what the cost to run it is, what your contingency plans are if you get sick, leave or get sued—and much more.

So how do you prepare for all that? How do you position your business to get the best valuation? How do you find investors? What information do you send them, and when they show interest, what do you say? What documents and expert advisors will you need to help you put it all together?

This section is about how to add value so investors will pay you more than what you paid. A lot more.

CHAPTER 9

Sell your vision

Vision is the art of seeing what is invisible to others
Jonathan Swift

When I was a kid in primary school, they made us read the book *A Fortunate Life* by A.B. Facey. If you've read the book, you'll know that life wasn't that fortunate for little Bert at all. But the moral of that book really stuck with me. Despite his desperately poor and violent upbringing, Bert genuinely believed that his life was fortunate; that the slings and arrows of misfortune that came his way were opportunities to be harnessed; and that happiness was not to be equated with pleasure or ease. I love that he managed to find great motivation from the difficulties in his life and I've taken inspiration from his story ever since.

I won't ever pretend that my life has been as hard as Bert's. It's been far from it. I've been quite blessed. I was born into a middle-class family in the leafy northern suburbs of Sydney and was very fortunate to grow up in an environment that valued education, endeavour and entrepreneurship. It's those beginnings that gave me the fire to launch my own company.

I remember being all of 10 years old and thinking, 'I want to own my own company!' Seriously, what kid of 10 thinks that? But I did. I saw my dad, in his nice suit and his shiny shoes, trundle off to work and I thought, like most boys of an impressionable age, 'I want to be like him'. I also remember him coming down the hallway with a cheque in his hand and his eyes shining, telling me he'd received it because of an investment he'd made that had turned out very well. I thought making money must be fun because he sure looked happy about receiving that cheque.

It's no secret that we disagreed on a lot of things, but like many fathers and sons who work together, we argued and then made up, argued again, made up, and so on. It wasn't an easy relationship, but we made it work and the sparks that flew helped us build a better business together.

My dad had his own successful accountancy practice, but he invested in pubs and was keenly interested in how they worked. He kept a tight rein on the finances of them, which is how I learned the tricks of the trade. I've learned some important lessons from my dad. Don't screw with people's money and pay people on time are two of them. When people don't get paid, they get very pissed off, and with good reason, so I've always made it my priority to ensure that people—staff, suppliers, investors—get paid on time.

How to get a better valuation

Unlike Dad, I actually worked in the pubs, not on them, and being the front man was what I enjoyed. We owned a pub together and we clashed regularly on how it should be run, but we always managed to work it out in the end and come out ahead. He wasn't that great with people and could often rub them up the wrong way.

One of the principles on which we disagreed was how money got spent. He never wanted to spend a thing on anything. I, however, believed you had to spend on something to get a result. For example, in 2013 we bought a pub in New South Wales called The CBD. I said to him at the outset, 'We need to spend $500 000 minimum on this to bring it up to speed'. The carpet was fraying, the chairs were broken, the paint was peeling.

'Why waste money on that?' he said. 'People are coming in, drinking, spending. Why reduce your profitability spending on stuff that people won't notice?'

'But they will Dad,' I would say. 'They will.' But he wouldn't have a bar of it, so we didn't spend the money.

Twelve months later, the customer numbers were way down, the profitability was shot and the place was on the brink of ruin.

I said to him, 'Can we start investing now? Can we start bringing this place back to what it was, and could be?'

He finally agreed.

I went to work. I did what I always did — which sounds easy but is pretty damn difficult to do in reality, especially on a tight time frame and even tighter budget — and that's to renovate. It was a very big pub — 1000 square metres on a 2000-square-metre block — which made it even more challenging.

The refurbished bistro at The CBD.

The refurbished hall at The CBD.

We moved the gaming room, upgraded the signage, laid new carpet, painted the walls, created a new menu, staged new events, launched new promotions, sent out media kits...and within a few months the place was pumping. At our open day, we sold 2600 schnitzels in one day! We won a fantastic commendation from the Australian Hotels Association and got extra media coverage for that, which in turn generated new customers for us, and so the virtuous cycle continued.

The profitability improved quickly and we could finally see the pub had turned the corner and was on the up. It was thrilling to see and incredibly gratifying to know the strategy and hard work had paid off.

Top 8 ways to increase value

We've renovated, refurbished and rebranded many pubs. We've made a lot of mistakes, but we've got a lot right and we now know what the formula for success looks like. Irrespective of what kind of retail business you have, take a look at the ways we increase the value of our pubs and how you can apply the same strategies to your business.

1. Change the menu or product offering to keep customers engaged.

2. Introduce a drinks menu or find a novel way to showcase existing products.

3. Play to the pub's strengths (e.g. if your demographic is young, host live music nights. If they're young families, install a playground to keep the kids entertained).

4. Introduce uniforms.

5. Employ really good staff who understand your values and ethos.

6. Tap into your local community.

7. Attend local community meetings.

8. Win awards.

That renovation paid off in more ways than one.

When I went to the bank to get the pub revalued, they could see that the disruption to trade had impacted our sales figures, but they could see what we were trying to do and didn't penalise us for this drop in trade. I presented them with the 'before and after' photos, the award we'd won, the increase in profitability and also a document outlining my track record of what I'd done with other pubs. All that combined served to create a vote of confidence from them and they not only approved the loan we asked for, but revalued the pub dramatically. The developers were interested too in what we'd done and could see the potential that we had made possible. My younger sister, who worked with Stockland at the time, introduced us to a developer she knew.

You can imagine our delight when they made us an offer we couldn't refuse. We bought the pub for $3.6 million in 2013 and, in 2015, we sold it to a consortium of developers for $6.25 million. Not bad for a few years' work. That's the power of reinvention.

Profit versus potential

My dad inadvertently taught me an invaluable lesson here. He taught me that you have to look at a business situation from many perspectives and try to see everyone's point of view. He was looking at it from one point of view: profitability. I was looking at it from another point of view: potential. This is the difference between an accountant and an entrepreneur. An accountant sees what is; an entrepreneur sees what could be. Both are important.

When I sell any pub now, I work hard to see it from multiple perspectives, particularly that of the property developer. They ask, 'Is it located on a high street or busy corner with plenty of pedestrian foot traffic?' 'Is it located close to a shopping centre with plenty of passing cars?' 'Are there sporting grounds, schools and office blocks nearby that will provide a steady source of trade during the day and night, on weekdays and weekends?' 'What competition is in the area?' 'What is the zoning regulation, and could the property be converted into a combination of residential and commercial elements?'

You must reinvest in your business

A business is like a tree. It needs to be watered, trimmed and fertilised. You need to spend money on it, plant it in the best position and ensure the soil is rich in nutrients so that it has the best opportunity to grow. A business is the same. You need to spend money on repairs, maintenance, upgrading equipment, reviewing the business model, changing the offering, keeping in touch with new and innovative elements—from the food and drinks you serve, to the technology you use to process orders or manage COVID-19 restrictions—you need to keep on top of everything.

It's easy to get left behind and not even know it. It's also easy to wallow in your own mediocrity without even realising it. Sometimes you need an outside eye to tell you what you're not seeing. When was the last time you asked an outside observer to assess your business? Have you ever invited your customers to be candid with you about what they think of your logo, website, customer service, premises, signage, staff? Their response could be illuminating, and not in a good way.

There's only one way to find out what customers and prospects think about you, and that's to ask.

WHAT ARE YOU NOT SEEING?

I remember when I was living in London with a few mates in a share house in Earls Court. We survived on instant noodles and cheap curries but were having a blast living in this mecca of bars, pubs and clubs. I had the front room, which—unfortunately for the passers-by—had no curtains or blinds so they could see me at all times of the night or day. I hoisted an old, torn, green sheet onto the pelmet to act as a curtain and give me some privacy from the passers-by. It was meant to be a stop-gap measure until I could find the time to get a proper blind installed.

After a few weeks I promptly forgot about the green sheet being a make-shift blind and got on with my life. When my girlfriend came to visit, she stood out the front of the house and said to me, 'When are you going to get rid of this torn green sheet as a blind?' 'What torn green sheet?' I said. 'The one that you're using as a blind right there,' she said, pointing at the window. I had completely forgotten that the sheet was even there. To my eye, it had become my curtain and I no longer saw it for what it truly was. An old green sheet. What are you no longer seeing? What have you become accustomed to? What are you overlooking that customers aren't?

The best way to see a business from multiple points of view is to conduct a 'pre-mortem'. Here's how it works, why it works and an example of how it helped us get through some COVID-19-related challenges.

Pre-mortems can help prevent failure

We're all familiar with post-mortems. We see them on TV shows like *CSI* where a white-coated medical professional wields a scalpel and cuts into the corpse of the deceased to find out what happened, when and why.

When a business dies, a similar process occurs. An administrator with a financial scalpel cuts into the corpse of the business to identify what happened, when and why.

Both types of post-mortems have value, but they don't alter the sad fact that the 'patient' has passed away. But what if we did things differently, before the post-mortem was needed? What if we conducted a pre-mortem on the business before it died so that we can predict what might go wrong *before* it goes wrong? Could that be useful?

I've been using pre-mortems in my business for decades now, and they are a powerful management tool that helps my team identify why a project or business has failed. We then work backwards to determine what could have led to that failure. The concept was created by a group of academics. Deborah J. Mitchell of the Wharton School, Jay Russo of Cornell and Nancy Pennington of the University of Colorado. As noted in Harvard Business Review, the researchers discovered that 'prospective hindsight—imagining that an event has already occurred—increased the ability to correctly identify reasons for future outcomes by 30%'.

If I can minimise my risk of failure by 30 per cent simply by imagining what could go wrong, that's a good use of my time. (I think about what could go wrong all the time anyway, so I may as well use the angst for a good purpose.)

The essence of a pre-mortem is that you don't wait for the business to fail before you examine it. You act 'as if' the business has already failed and then you work backwards to unpick the events that could lead to failure and install solutions so that it doesn't happen in the first place.

I often get asked, 'Is a pre-mortem the same as Edward de Bono's "black hat" brainstorming session?' Not quite. Those sessions are predicated on asking team members what might go wrong; the pre-mortem operates on the assumption that the 'patient' has died, and so asks what did go wrong as if the disaster has already occurred.

There are dozens of things that can go wrong with a business. Some of them will be under your control, others won't. It's important to summarise them all because while you can't control external influences and situations, the very act of thinking about them and predicting what could happen helps you create strategies for mitigating the damage they could cause.

HOW A PRE-MORTEM HELPED US DURING LOCKDOWN

During the COVID-19 lockdown, our pubs were shut for around two months. That's a hell of a lot of time for a business that trades 24/7, 365 days to be shut. Like all businesses, we were haemorrhaging money. Rent, wages, stock — and more. But because we'd already done disaster scenario planning via our pre-mortem workshops, we were as prepared as any for what lay ahead.

We relied heavily on our Real Time Management Reporting (RTMR) systems (more on these shortly) to help us model a range of scenarios to see if the numbers stacked up. For example, we ran the numbers to answer the questions that everyone was posing at the time. Should we open for a few hours a day, or not at all? Should we offer take-away meals and coffee or just coffee? What about home deliveries? Would that work? If so, how much staff and stock would we need? Would it be worth it? What about our responsibility to the community? What role should a community pub play in keeping people united?

Our modelling helped us make fast, accurate decisions as to what we should do next, which was stay open and offer take-aways and home deliveries. We invested deeply in digitising the business even further and conducted remote training sessions with our staff to teach them how to deal with this 'new normal'. Keeping up with the ever-changing nature of the pandemic was a full-time job in itself, but due to the systems and

(continued)

strategies we'd put in place, we were able to weather the storm better than most because we could communicate with everyone on our team quickly, efficiently and accurately.

In times of stress, business owners often cut back, which is normal. We do the opposite. We step up. We kept advertising, we kept up all our social media channels, we invested further with our staff and offered all of them access to the Employment Assistance Program, where they could access free counselling. They were awesome throughout. I was conscious that they had mortgages, families and financial commitments to cover and worked hard to keep them all engaged. To my surprise and delight, most of them offered to stand down during the time, or to take part-time wages, leave or long service leave so as not to impact the business too much during this difficult time. It was incredibly moving to see my team rally like that to support not just the business they worked for, but me. Loyalty is a two-way street. If you look after your team, they'll look after you. Conversely, if you don't look after them, then expect the same treatment in return.

Our customers appreciated it too. When we returned to normal trading, sales were higher than ever, but the goodwill and customer feedback we received from our patrons for staying open was magnified. Here's a note we received from a customer: 'You travelled 10 kilometres to deliver me a pizza. I can't tell you what that meant to me. I live on my own and just seeing another person, the delivery driver, when I hadn't seen a person for weeks, really lifted my spirits. Thank you.'

The value of real-time reports and why they matter

People often ask us how we can make pubs work when others can't: how we can extract a profit from a sector when others are losing money hand over fist. There are many reasons for our success, but one of them is due to my insistence on and discipline with creating real-time reports.

Now before you head off into snooze land at the thought of a deep dive into reports, just know that getting real-time, accurate data is the key to the success of every business. Look at Kogan, the online retailer that became a billion-dollar sensation when it listed on the Australian Stock Exchange in 2016. One of the reasons it's been so successful is because it was an early exponent of dynamic pricing. What does this mean? It means that before it lists a product and its price, the software does an electronic sweep of the internet for all the current prices of that product, and then presents the customer with the best price at that particular time of the day. That price may change in a few hours or even a few minutes, but it's calibrated to be the best price at that moment.

We're not an e-commerce business with thousands of products available for sale 24/7 so we don't need that level of complexity to work out our pricing, but just as Kogan assesses multiple factors to determine a price, so do we. Those factors are simple in nature but you'd be surprised at how many business owners fail to even know the most basic numbers that sit behind their key business decisions, such as pricing. They don't know what they've sold, when, for how much, how often, what it cost, what the gross profit was and much more. We know all that and more about our products and services, and importantly, my managers know it too. Data is useless if it doesn't get into the hands of the right people, at the right time—and the right people are my staff and the right time is daily.

Real reports in real time for real people

Our system is called Real Time Management Reporting (RTMR). It enables us to make decisions about products, people or processes very quickly. The result? We don't have to rely on gut instinct, experience or random factors to make important decisions. We make them based on cold, hard facts. It also helps me delegate because if my people are trained correctly—and I make sure they are—they can make the right decisions without my input.

For any business owner wanting to scale, this kind of reporting is the holy grail. It's taken me 30 years of working in pubs to become an overnight success, but that hands-on experience, combined with my formal education—including an MBA and a Graduate Certificate in Applied Finance, and other degrees and diplomas—has enabled me to funnel that knowledge into designing these customised reports for my staff, which permits them to function independently without my direct oversight. This means I can get on with working *on* the business, not *in* the business, and for me, working on the business means looking ahead, identifying trends, sourcing investors, building teams and finding the best way to give investors an extraordinary rate of return on their investment.

What's in a name?

I used to call these real-time reports 'Steve's Reports' and they'd go out to our team on a daily basis. I did consider renaming the reports based on the people they were going to, so that Johnno would get 'Johnno's Reports' and Casey would 'Casey's Reports', and so on.

I realised pretty quickly though that this personalisation of reports wouldn't work. It was a subtle thing, but when Johnno, for example, got his report with his name on it, the risk would be that he'd think the report was for him, and his eyes only, and that he could set it aside and not do anything with it.

Keeping it as 'Steve's Reports' would reinforce the fact that they were indeed Steve's Reports for Johnno: that I expected him to review the reports and act on them.

I'm very easy going about many things, but incredibly disciplined when it comes to some things, and reporting is one of them. My team know that those reports *must* go out at the same time every day and that this schedule cannot be altered. My staff have come to expect them, and even enjoy receiving them (who'd have thought: a report that people actually enjoy receiving?) mainly because it helps them make good decisions in a complex and ever-changing environment.

Why the 'rules of thumb' don't always apply

These real-time reports help us rely less on assumptions and instinct and make decisions based on fact. When my family and friends failed to come up with the $1 million to help me buy The Rutherford, I learned a valuable lesson, and that was to *never assume anything*. Assuming can get you into a whole world of trouble. It nearly bankrupted me.

Just as you should never assume anything, you should also never assume that the 'rules of thumb' always apply. The rule of thumb is a generally accepted guideline, policy or method of doing something based on practice rather than facts.

When we follow the rule of thumb without really doing the due diligence that's needed to make a qualified decision, we can be lulled into believing something is true when it isn't. If we base subsequent decisions on this erroneous fact, it leads to more bad decisions getting made. Before you know it, the proverbial has hit the fan and you don't know why or how it happened.

I see this happen in my industry all the time and it's a very fast way to lose money quickly. Here's an example.

NEVER RELY ON THE 'RULE OF THUMB'

My mate Brownie owns a pub in the middle of Sydney's CBD. He wanted to stimulate sales in his hotel bottle shop, so went to see what a very successful hotelier was doing across town in his bottle shop. He noticed that they'd dropped their prices of a six-pack of beer by 30 per cent. He assumed this was a winning strategy so he followed suit and dropped his prices too.

It didn't work. Sales remained the same, but the strategy unleashed three unintended (and unfortunate) consequences. It reduced his profit margin, set up a false expectation of what his customers could expect in the future and made it really hard for him to restore the beer to its original price point. It was a woeful experiment all because he assumed that if the strategy worked for one pub, it would work for his.

Suburban restaurants and cafés succumb to the rule of thumb all the time. They see the sandwich shop across the road offer a bacon and egg roll with coffee for $9 so they price the same roll at $8. The tactic fails, they lose money and they wonder why. It's because they were basing their assumptions on faulty logic. They assumed that those customers would cross the street to take up a cheaper offer. They might, but people don't always do the logical thing. Maybe they had a loyalty card with the first café. Maybe they knew the café owner and didn't want to be disloyal. Maybe they were elderly and didn't want to cross the busy road.

The rule of thumb comes into play for us when we need to decide if we should raise our prices. For example, the federal government raises the alcohol excise tax twice a year. This is a big impost for us and we have to carefully weigh up whether to pass on the costs to the customer. People often ask us why we don't pass on this small increase. The answer is best explained by asking a question. As a savvy business owner, what would you prefer: 65 per cent gross profit on $0; or 65 per cent gross profit on $1? We look for other ways to maintain the margins—for example, we work with stakeholders to see what deals we can do to keep the customers happy.

We know our customers, and we know that if they buy one drink (at the price they are accustomed to) they are more than likely to buy another drink. After all, who has one drink at the pub and goes home? The logic behind this is simple. It's easier to get people to buy a second drink than to buy the first, so while we may lose some margin on the first schooner, we make it up on the second.

These are the tiny, yet important decisions all business owners have to make when setting prices and deciding on what costs do or don't get passed on to the customers. It's an intricate dance and you get it wrong at your peril. We operate on razor-thin margins and one wrong move can set us back dramatically. That's why you really have to do your due diligence, know your costs of goods and dig deep to get into the nitty gritty of how a price increase will impact not just the first sale, but subsequent sales too.

Following the rule of thumb is not a great strategy for making important decisions. Doing so can easily lead to quick losses. Simply put: don't assume that what everyone else is doing will work for you. Do your research; look at your customer demographic; delve into the data and then make your decision.

Making cents of the profit and loss

It will come as no surprise to you to know that I think the profit and loss statement is one of the most powerful management tools any business can have. If you haven't already familiarised yourself with this report, make haste and do so as it's the beating heart behind your business.

I've had many a debate with some top accountants about how to tweak gross profit *here* and wage percentages *there*; and how if we adjusted the prices *here*, we could increase sales *there*, which would result in this business increasing in value by *this* much, while the other business would increase in value by *that* much. While it's an entertaining conversation to have (for people like me who love playing with figures), it can descend into an intellectualised debate because for all those numbers and assumptions to align and be useful, you're relying on the business maintaining the same quantity of sales and the same level of expenses, and expecting the customers to do exactly the same thing every day— which of course they don't. It's enough to drive you to drink!

So, you have to get back to basics, work with what you have and know and make it your daily aim to do what you do well with what you have. To do that, you need to get back to basics. You might be interested in knowing what factors we track and what our reports look like. No matter what business you're in, these are the kinds of reports everyone can use and benefit from. Here are a few of the factors we track on a daily basis:

- sales
- purchases
- gross profit
- wages
- cash flow.

Tracking these variables is pretty simple to do, but you'd be surprised at how few businesses actually do it. I don't know how you can't measure them: if you don't, how do you know what you're doing? Get the basics right by analysing the data and you'll find that a lot of the decision making will be done for you.

Cash flow is king

While cash flow is last on my list above, it must get looked at first. Many business owners overlook this factor at their peril, because while they might obsess about their profit and loss statement, they don't pay enough attention to when bills are coming up, or whether there's enough cash in the bank to pay them.

For those new to business, you might be wondering, what even is cash flow? Cash flow is simply a projection of your sales and when invoices are due. It's a measure of the fluidity of your business and helps you plan ahead so that you don't get caught short of cash. Nothing is more stressful than thinking you're having a good month, quarter or year, only to realise you've got a stomping great tax bill that needs to be paid—and it needs to be paid next week.

We've all seen the nightly news on TV where the famous business owner falls from grace for failing to pay their tax bill and is paraded through the courts to meet their ignominious fate. This sad end to an otherwise illustrious business career is often caused by the fact they did not set aside enough cash to pay their tax bill. They either didn't think to do so, or chose not to, deciding they would pay the tax bill later. Before they know it, the next tax bill arrives, they can't pay it and within a very short period of time, their cumulative tax bill becomes insurmountable. This causes incredible stress to the business owner, so much so that they stop focusing on running the business and start focusing on how they can either pay down their tax bill or find an unscrupulous way to avoid paying more tax. This vicious cycle continues and voilà! There they are on the nightly news, their reputation in tatters. All because they didn't understand the importance of cash flow.

Build a relationship with your banker

To manage cash flow, it really helps to have good relationships with all your strategic partners and your suppliers so that you know what your terms of trade are and how long you have before payments become due. It's important to be able to communicate quickly with them if you can't make those terms. If you can control these factors, you're controlling your business—not the other way around.

If you find yourself in this situation, the best—and sometimes the only—thing to do is to come clean. Ring the bank, tell them the situation you're in, ask for their help and organise a payment plan to pay down the debt. Most banks will appreciate you being upfront with them and will help you get back on track—and they have special loan schemes to help you pay back a tax debt with very manageable interest rates. This is why it pays to have a relationship with your banker. If they already know you, trust you and can see you have a good track record, they're more likely to work with you to help you get through it. Having a relationship will not only help you get through this rough patch, it will potentially smooth the path for any future loans or financing you may need.

Banks don't like to take risks on anything, and anyone who has an unpaid tax debt will not be looked upon favourably when applying for a loan.

How credit departments work (and why it takes forever to get a loan approved)

Do you know why it takes banks so long to approve a loan application? It's because so many people and departments within the bank look at your application. It moves through multiple hands and each of them looks at it very carefully, assessing it against a whole range of measures you may not be aware of. Tax debt is one of them.

The bank's credit department is generally broken into tiers: from residential lending (up to $3 million) to small business lending ($3 million– $50 million) right through to institutional lending ($50 million+). Each tier has the ability to approve an application for a certain amount. Once the amount tips over into another band, a new set of rules and lending criteria apply. Your application will generally be managed by one person and they'll monitor its progress. While this person won't (generally) lose their job if they lend money to someone who doesn't pay it back, they will be hauled over the coals and interrogated as to why they loaned out the money and it won't be a pleasant day at the office for that person. That's a long way of saying that your loan application gets looked at carefully by real people, in real time, and that having a personal relationship with your bank can be of enormous help. If they know you, have talked to you, understand your situation and trust you, they'll be more likely to give you the benefit of the doubt.

Dashboards rule

While real-time reports are good, having a weekly dashboard that focuses on the key elements of your business is even better. Dashboards need to take into account the variable costs and revenues so that you can keep tabs on these anomalies. And don't worry too much if the dashboard doesn't show a positive sign every week. You may have a big, one-off expense coming in (like a renovation or a tax bill) or have to pay an electricity bill this week that won't arise for another quarter. Sales, of course, will fluctuate depending on the season too, but by monitoring these on a weekly basis you can start to see the trends and spot any outliers that could be threatening you in the future. You definitely want to keep tabs on expenses because if they blow out, you need to be able to act quickly to bring them under control.

Celebrate your success

And don't forget to reward yourself at the end of the quarter (your data will tell you if you are deserving of the reward, of course) so that you get to enjoy the fruits of your labour. Remember why you're in business to start with, which is to have control over your time, freedom to do what you want and the independence to forge your own path. When times get tough and things aren't going well, it's really easy to lose sight of why you started the business in the first place and what you were trying to achieve. Sometimes that desk job in the open-plan office with the 45-minute lunch break and the 5 pm knock-off starts to look really attractive and you wonder whether you made the right decision by leaving the security of working for someone else and whether it would be easier to just give it all up, chuck it in and go back to the normal life you had before.

I have one word for you: don't. Hang in there. The juice is worth the squeeze. For me, and for you too, I assume (or else you wouldn't be reading this book), the freedom to do what you want, when you want, is the holy grail of why we run our own businesses. While running your own business may not always be plain sailing, and it may require working long hours and dealing with stress and fatigue, there is one thing I'm sure of: I'd rather work 100 hours for myself than 50 hours for someone else.

Summing up...

1. You need to reinvest in your business. Do it before you need to.

2. Business valuations can be impacted by how you present your business to the bank. Take the time to craft your presentation.

3. Are you too close to your business to see how others see it? Ask customers, colleagues or trusted advisors for their honest opinions.

4. Conduct a 'pre-mortem' before you embark on any major project, purchase, acquisition or campaign to spot potential points of failure.

5. Invest in sourcing real-time data and give your team access to it to help them make informed decisions.

6. 'Rules of thumb' don't always apply.

7. If you can't read a profit and loss statement, enrol in a course to find out how.

8. Build a personal relationship with your banker. You're more likely to be given the 'benefit of the doubt' if they can put a face to your name.

9. If you get behind with your bank repayments or paying a tax bill, let the bank know before they ring you.

CHAPTER 10
Sell your story

> **The mirror is a worthless invention. The only way to truly see yourself is in the reflection of someone else's eyes.**
> *Voltaire*

What do you call an investment manager who will only invest a minimum of $50 million? Your best friend.

That's a joke, sort of. But if you're going to seek out an investment, you may as well seek out those who can invest a significant amount of money. After all, it takes almost as much work to secure $15 000 as it does $15 million, so you may as well focus your efforts and go for gold at the start.

The first thing they are going to ask for is some information about the business. You'll remember from Chapter 8 that the document they'll want to see is the information memorandum (IM).

The IM is where you get to set out your vision for the business and why someone should invest in you. It's a very important document and any competent investor will ask for it, review it carefully, get their lawyers and accountants to pore over it as well and hold you to account.

It's the document that summarises your dream and it tells investors (and your banker) what the business will do, what it will sell, who to, for how much, why it's different from others, what's in it for them to invest—and much more.

How to create an IM that impresses investors

When I started out, I had no idea what an IM was. I made a few mistakes and lost a bit of money because of that. I do things differently now and the IM is at the heart of every investor pitch I make. It's also the starting point for when I invest in a business.

The IM serves many purposes. It's there to help you and your team keep track of what you're doing, but it's a very important document that shows the bankers and investors what you're up to, what you've got in store and if you're worth investing in. It tells your story.

It's also a document that helps get people excited about what you plan to do. It's where your dreams and visions are recorded; it's where your passion and love for the business you're about to build come alive and it's where you get to share all that enthusiasm with everyone around you. You'll definitely need the input of your accountant and lawyer to bring this plan to fruition, but it's worth the investment. One good plan could generate millions in investment so take the time and effort to make it both accurate and attractive.

If you're selling a business, or sourcing investors, here's a starting point for what you need to put in your IM so that you increase your chances of success.

The IM has seven main components:

1. your history as a businessperson

2. a summary of your team

3. a description of your asset(s)

4. financials and projections

5. structure

6. risks

7. application form.

Your history as a businessperson

While all investors are not the same, what they have in common is they want to know who's running the business. (That's you, by the way.) You're the leader here, even if it's just you (and your cat). If the business has no track record, sales, clients or history, then they'll be very keen to know more about you since that's who they'll be investing in. They'll want to know about your passion for the product, your experience in the industry and why you love working in that sector. They'll also want to know about your past experiences: your successes, failures, the risks you've taken, the challenges you've faced and the strategies you've applied to deal with those challenges.

If investors are nervous investing with you, or they don't know you well enough to trust you, you can use your past success stories to flag how you'll deal with future challenges. They need some form of comfort to get them over the line, and showcasing how you've dealt with problems in the past can be the ticket to success. Have your stories ready to go as you'll never know when you need to tell them.

I recall a time when I was doing a national roadshow to raise money for the pub fund. I was meeting with a raft of family offices and high-net-worth individuals, but it didn't go to plan.

HOW TO REASSURE NERVOUS INVESTORS

I had 20 meetings lined up with potential investors over two days. I was in the lift going up to the 25th floor of one of Sydney's most prestigious office

(continued)

towers. As the lift went up, I glanced at the TV screen in the lift. There was breaking news: the Australian stock market had just crashed — a Black Friday of sorts — and it was widely reported that this was one of the worst days in Australia's stock-market history. My heart sank. If I was hearing this, it meant that the investment advisors I was about to meet would also have heard it. Not only would they personally have probably lost a stack of money on the stock market, but their clients would almost certainly have lost money too. No doubt they were on the phone to those investment advisors right now, trying to establish what they had lost. When this happens, most investment advisors go into defensive mode, trying to stem the losses, desperate to get out of whatever negative position they are in. To put it mildly, it wasn't a great time to be pitching an investment opportunity to a conservative family business.

My first thought was to cancel the meeting and come back another time after the dust had settled. But that thought lasted a microsecond because I also knew that I never give up, I never give in and I always see the best in the situation I'm in. Mud. Lotus.

As the lift reached the top of the building, I decided to change the pitch I had planned to give. Instead of telling them about what I had planned for the future, I decided to tell them how I had managed tough times like this in the past. Keeping flexible in times like this is critical. Things don't always go to plan and you need to be nimble on your feet so you can move and adapt to the situation at hand.

I knew the word 'recession' would be on the top of their mind so I reflected back to the recession of 2008, which I had experienced. I spoke of how we took the gutsy approach of actually spending money during the recession, when everyone else in our industry was tightening their belt. I spoke of how we renovated one of our pubs and how that led to a 30 per cent increase in turnover. I talked about how we changed our business model to adapt to the environment, such as offering specials on our meals, happy hours, launching customer promotions and encouraging existing customers to spend more.

I also spoke about the changes to legislation we had experienced over the years and the strategies we had implemented to deal with these. My industry is notoriously vulnerable to politicians creating new rules that have the potential to be devastating. I discussed the changes we had endured over the years and the results we had posted that demonstrated we were not only on top of it, we were ahead of it.

My strategy for revealing my ability to manage past challenges worked. I walked away that day with three investors, each investing millions on behalf of their high-net-worth family businesses. They also introduced me to a number of other investors, which is always my strategy: ask for more referrals, even if the people you're talking to don't buy in.

You must make every meeting an opportunity to find an introduction to another potential investor.

Be enthusiastic

Whether you're pitching for investor funds or interviewing for a role, show some passion. Don't be afraid to show enthusiasm. I've often interviewed staff for a new role and while internally they're keen to win it, the enthusiasm hasn't reached their face. As a result, they come across as too cool for school, ambivalent about their desire to work with us and almost nonchalant as to whether they get the job or not. While no-one expects you to be doing somersaults to showcase your passion for the job, we do want to see enthusiasm, interest, passion and energy for the job we're offering. It's the same when you're pitching for investors. They want to know you're excited to have them on board, that they matter and that you will work hard for them.

Failure is your friend

As counterintuitive as this may seem, don't be afraid to talk about past failures because most sophisticated investors know that success is often born from failure. Having said that, don't go bragging about your failures because that won't impress anyone. But if you get asked about the failures you've had, don't say 'none' because it's probably not true, and if it is, it won't win you any kudos from the investors as they'll think you're too green to manage their money.

If you do need to talk about your failures, frame them positively as a learning experience and be clear about how you'll bring those lessons to this new endeavour. Some investors will only invest in business owners who have already failed. A famous Australian entrepreneur, the founder of a billion-dollar tech firm, spectacularly lost $20 million of investors' money on one of his earlier forays. His future investors were happy with that result (mainly because it wasn't their money) because they knew they'd benefit from that $20 million 'education'.

A summary of your team

In addition to knowing about you, investors will also want to know who's in your team. They'll want to invest in a strong management team with a good track record in their industry. If you have a team, this is what they'll want to know:

- Who are they and what role will they play?

- Who have they worked for in the past?

- Who reports to whom? (You can insert an organisational chart to showcase this.)

- Who is the second in command (2IC) and what succession plan have you put in place?

- What are your growth plans?

- What markets or new products will you expand into?

- What is the time frame for that expansion?

- What will you spend the investors' money on?

- How long do you expect the business to last?

- What are your exit strategies?

YOUR TEAM IS BIGGER THAN YOU THINK

When I get asked about my team, I don't just talk about the team who currently work with me. I talk about the people I have worked with in the past, what they taught me, the successes we achieved together and the results of those collaborations. For example, I've worked for some of the best pub operators in the business. These wonderful people taught me everything there is to know about running multi-pub venues so when I'm asked who is on my team, I don't just reference my current team, I reference all those who have guided and influenced me along the way. They are all part of my 'team'.

If you are just starting out and you don't have a 'team' to speak of, don't hesitate to mention any business advisors you work with as part of your team. It could be your accountant, bookkeeper, lawyer, graphic designer, marketer, web developer: all these people help you run the business, so they are part of your team and can legitimately be mentioned in the IM. Obviously, you'll need their permission to be included in any documentation, but they are all part of the network that helps you do what you do.

When I create my IMs, I always reference my accountants, lawyers and other trusted partners as part of my team, simply because they are! While they're not employees, they're like partners to me and their involvement in the business is critical to its success.

Description of your asset(s)

This is where you describe the physical asset of what you're offering. For us, this is where we describe the actual hotel or pub we're buying or renovating. Our investors need to know the location, the physical size of the property, how many people it seats, the number of bars, accommodation rooms, gaming machines, what local infrastructure is nearby (shopping centres, movie theatres, football stadiums, schools, etc.), the car park capacity, and so on. We'll also discuss the developments in the area, such as new housing developments, road constructions and freeway extensions.

If you're fundraising to finance a renovation or refurbishment, describe the plans you have and, if possible, include any drawings or renderings from the architect as this will make it easier to sell your proposition. You should also include a set of financials that detail the extra sales, revenue and profit that the renovation will generate.

Financials and projections

This part of the plan is where you list all your financials, such as your profit and loss statements, balance sheets and also projections. They'll want to know the detail behind your sales projections, revenue, expected returns and the time frames for these returns.

You would have done some projections with your accountant on what the business will make and from this you will work out what you can comfortably pay investors.

While it's tempting to get ahead of yourself and get excited about the potential, it's always best to under-promise and over-perform. Investors like to know what they're getting into and it's easier to manage an investor who has received the return they expected than to justify why you didn't reach the expectation you promised. Be conservative.

If you aren't already acquainted with your profit and loss statement and balance sheet, ask your accountant to take you through it — or even better, enrol in a short course at TAFE or with the local council and learn the basics of how to read your financial statements. It'll be money well spent.

Here's a sample profit and loss statement. Generally speaking, it's good to provide three years' worth of projections.

Gross profit	**$620 000**
Gross profit %	*62.00%*
Other income	
Accommodation income	$22 000
Commissions	$30 000
Gaming income	$345 000
Miscellaneous income	$3 000
Rebates	$27 000
Total other income	**$427 000**
TOTAL INCOME	**$1 047 000**
Operating expenses	
Administration costs	$33 000
Employment costs	$390 000
Financial and legal expenses	$10 000
Occupancy costs	$54 000
General expenses	$280 000
Total operating expenses	**$767 000**
Earnings before interest, tax and depreciation	**$280 000**

Plan for contingencies

A word from the wise: factor into your plan any contingency that could impact the plan so that if it does happen, you're prepared. A leaky roof, litigation, floods or fire can all have a massive impact on your cash flow, disrupt trade and reduce your ability to meet your financial goals and upend your projections. The cash flow required to get through these events needs to be factored into your financials. Yes, you hope they don't happen, and on balance, they won't, but what we want and what actually happens are two different things. If you want to sleep easy at night, keep your investors happy and minimise surprises, nominate the contingencies, cost them out, factor them in so you can put them out of your mind and put your energy into focusing on growing the business.

HOW TO PROTECT YOUR BUSINESS FROM FIRES, FLOODS, ROBBERIES (AND DEATHS)

If you're in business for as long as I've been, you'll experience pretty much everything life has to throw at you. I've had floods, fires, deaths, robberies, litigation—and more. The flood we had was caused by a burst water main that flooded our cellar, cool room and carpet, ruined our stock and shorted the electrics throughout the pub. We've even had people die on our premises. Fortunately, we had insurance which covered those costs and the loss of trade. All this needs to be considered when you take out insurance. Get an expert in your sector to give you an insurance quote as they'll know what needs to be insured and how much it's worth. They'll help you spot important clauses that could make all the difference when it comes time to claim. Your industry association or peak body will have recommendations for who you can contact.

Structure

There are many ways to structure your business. This must be done with the input of your accountant as they can see the benefits, costs and risks of the various structures. The structure you decide on will be determined by the stage of growth you're at. For example, if your business is expanding rapidly and you generate more than $2 million within a 12-month period, this may trigger certain corporate laws and may mean you need a trustee. If you have more than 20 investors, you may also need a trustee, so make sure you engage an accountant and a lawyer who can give you the best advice for your situation.

The 7 most popular business structures

1. Sole proprietorship

2. Limited partnership

3. Corporation

4. Limited liability company (LLC)

5. Non-profit organisation

6. Cooperative

7. Trust

Risks

Investors don't like surprises. Any. Ever. Especially when they impact their return on investment. That's why it's vital that you outline any and all risks that they may face if they invest with you at the start. It could be legislative changes, increased competition in the area, a new tax or even a pandemic! (Who saw that coming?)

One of the fastest ways to work out what might go wrong is to focus on the riskiest assumptions. These are the factors that could send you reeling. We use our pre-mortems to identify them and then work backwards to see how we can mitigate this risk. Here are a few events we cover off when conducting our pre-mortems:

- What if an investor wants to exit?

- What if a cashed-up competitor sets up a rival pub in our area?

- What if a key employee gets poached by a competitor?

- What if the government changes the legislation?

It's worth documenting the risks your business faces. You'll need to account for them in an investor pitch at some point so you may as well get brainstorming now.

A lot of my mates work in the start-up sector and have to deal with these kinds of riskiest assumptions:

- What if our whiz-bang chief technology officer, who developed our code, leaves and takes the source code to a competitor?

- What if the celebrity we've hired to spruik our company has a fall from grace — or worse, gets arrested for breaking the law?

- What if our preferred social media platform 'cancels' us and deletes all our followers?

- What if our biggest client walks away?

- What if our data gets hacked?

- What if interest rates go up?

- What if our key client doesn't pay their invoice?

These are just a few of the scenarios worth planning for so you can put your best foot forward, secure those investors with confidence and have the highest chance of succeeding.

Some investors will want to know how you dealt with COVID-19. Have your stories prepared. Few industries have suffered more than hospitality and events. But now that we're living with it, I work hard to share with my investors how we're managing it. They're worried about how their investment will be impacted so we need to keep them fully informed of what we're doing now, and what we plan to do moving forward. We can't change the fact we have COVID in our midst, but what we can do is be on the front foot to ensure they know what we're doing to protect their investment.

Expand with caution

While you'll never want to actively reject investment or decline the opportunity to build your business quickly, sometimes it's better to expand slowly so that you're educating yourself on the do's and don'ts as you grow. On the other hand, if you have an aggressive time frame for expansion and domination, and you don't have the requisite experience to manage that growth and all it entails, make sure your advisors are briefed correctly and understand your growth strategy so they can help you make the right decisions.

Application form

This is the document that seals the deal. If the investor is keen to proceed, this is the document they complete to indicate their intent to invest, how much they want to invest, how they can transfer the funds, the key dates they need to be aware of, contact details for us and our team—and much more. Once the funds have been received, you will need to send the investor a Share Certificate that summarises how many shares they have bought and a timeline for completion of the transaction.

Take note of Murphy's law here and know that this process will take longer than you think, cost more than you think and be more complicated than you think, so give yourself plenty of time to make it all come together.

Go big or go home

As we've seen, it takes as much effort to secure a small investment as a large investment, so if you're going to seek out an investment, go big or go home. Think big, dream large and ask for as much as you think your investor can afford because the paperwork, the meetings and the responsibilities that you will undertake will be the same no matter how much they put in. In some ways, taking a small investment from an investor can be more of a headache than taking a big investment. Some investors can tend to overstate their importance, want to get involved with the day-to-day running of the business or expect rights and responsibilities that are not deserving of that level of investment. Set the rules from the outset and let them know what you'll be reporting and when. Try to seek out larger investment amounts because it will mean you have to report to fewer investors and can focus on doing the work that needs to be done, which is growing the business.

Top 5 things you never say to investors

1. 'I'm pretty sure it will go okay.'

2. 'You've got plenty of money.'

3. 'We will go broke if we don't get your funding.'

4. 'I want to retire as soon as I can.'

5. 'There's nothing wrong with having a beer at 8 in the morning—it's 12 o'clock somewhere!'

Additional documents your investors may want to see

There's other documentation you can provide that will demonstrate to the investors or buyers that you know what you're doing, take the process seriously and understand the gravity of what is at stake.

Confidentiality

You may want to send your potential investors a non-disclosure agreement (NDA) to protect any intellectual property that you own and to deter those who hear your ideas from stealing them. It can feel awkward to ask a high-net-worth individual to sign a document to protect your idea, but you must treat your idea with respect, no matter how fledgling it may be.

Most sophisticated investors are familiar with NDAs, don't have an issue with signing them and may potentially respect you for having the confidence to back yourself and take steps to protect your idea. After all, if you're asking them to invest their money in your idea, they want to know that you're being prudent in protecting the very thing that will deliver them a great return. You can find a standard NDA on the internet, but like most legal documents, you get what you pay for, so take the time to run it by a legal professional to ensure you're protected. That's why people pay lawyers: it buys you protection and shifts the burden of responsibility onto the lawyer to ensure that you're being protected. (By the way, try not to send a 30-page NDA to the investor. That will just annoy them and flag that you're a novice at this. Two or three pages should be sufficient.)

Constitution

The constitution is the playbook your investment vehicle must play by. You'll recall from chapter 2 that the constitution I had with my fund was faulty and nearly cost me my business, so I had to change it. I needed 100 per cent of the investors to vote on any expenditure, which was clearly unworkable because we would have needed to get approval for even the smallest of purchases. If an investor had said 'no' to a change, that would have put the fund, and me, in a very difficult position. They could prevent the fund from making progress or even ask to be bought out at a higher price, creating a stalemate and freezing the fund from expanding.

Management contract

Someone needs to run the company and that someone is probably you. As the managing director, you'll need to be paid a fee to run the company and be accountable for a whole range of performance measures. This agreement is often called a management contract; it's made between you and the board of directors and will include the following:

- *definitions:* an outline of what everything in the contract means so that there is no misunderstanding

- *fees:* what you'll be paid

- *key duties:* an outline of the specific duties you will perform

- *annual review:* when it will take place and what it will involve

- *performance fees or bonuses:* details on what extra fees you'll be paid if you meet the required targets

- *your obligations:* what the board and investors expect you to do

- *the board's obligations:* what you and the investors can expect the board to do

- *remedies for dispute resolution:* strategies for how you, the board and others will resolve any disputes, disagreements or decisions that end in a stalemate

- *time frames:* a summary of when key activities need to take place.

HOW TO SPEAK 'LAWYER'

Lawyers are such fun people to work with. Not only do they charge you for opening an email, but when they're wrong, they'll try to make it look like it was your fault, and then charge you to fix it!

But in all seriousness, let me say this: a good lawyer is worth their weight in gold. If you have to go to court, you don't want a cut-rate lawyer representing you. The law is a very serious business and one wrong comma, full stop, missed word or incorrect assumption can cost you many millions, and possibly deprive you of your liberty. Like finding the right accountant, you'll need to shop around to find a good lawyer, but once you do, hold onto them because they will become your trusted advisor and a valued member of your team for many years to come.

Having said all that, let's have a bit of fun at their expense. As you can see, I've had a bit to do with lawyers, and if you're successful you probably will too. So it's worth understanding the language they speak. It's called 'legalese'. Here's an interpretive guide to ensure that when you next meet with a lawyer, you understand what they're saying.

When they say...	What they really mean is...
We can advise you against that but it's your decision.	Don't do it.
We can only offer legal advice.	We have no idea about the commercial side of the deal and the impacts your decision may make on the bottom line.
We don't make recommendations but we have dealt with that firm many times before and they are easy to deal with.	We recommend you use that firm.
We recommend you seek the services of...	We get a percentage of whatever they charge you.
We charge in six-minute increments.	When we start sending one-line email responses to your questions, we are robbing you blind.
We will have you put $x in a trust and will deduct from that fee as the invoices come in.	This is what we will be charging, so you won't see that Rembrandt again.
This requires serious consideration so we will come back to you as soon as practicable.	We are going to lunch and don't really care about the urgency of the situation you are in.
I will call to discuss.	I don't want to put that in writing because it is probably the wrong advice and I don't want to be sued over it.
Let's have an adult conversation about this.	We have fucked something up. We know you are angry and are trying to provoke you so you get angrier and miss the fact that we have fucked up.
I'm a lawyer! You can't speak to me that way!	I have a law degree and that gives me a God-given right to think I'm smarter than you, even though I don't know what I'm talking about in this situation.

Summing up...

1. If you want people to invest in your business, create an information memorandum (IM) and make it look impressive.

2. If you don't have a track record in your current industry, tell investors about your track record in your previous industry.

3. Frame past failures as examples of what you've learned and demonstrate how you'll bring that knowledge and experience to your next venture.

4. Your suppliers and professional advisors can be presented as 'members of your team'. Get their permission first to be named though.

5. Be enthusiastic. Investors will be impressed by your energy and passion.

6. Investors don't like surprises. Plan for contingencies and factor them into your projections.

7. Get insurance and find an expert in your sector to guide you on the exact insurances you need.

8. Expand with caution.

9. Don't forget to attach an application form to your IM. Signing this is how investors signal their interest.

10. It takes as much effort to secure a $15000 investment as it does a $15 million investment. Aim high to start with.

11. Don't ask investors to sign a lengthy non-disclosure agreement (NDA). Two or three pages should suffice.

12. You'll need a good lawyer. Choose one who has experience in your industry.

13. Ask your industry association for a referral to a lawyer with expertise in your sector.

14. When you find a good lawyer, hold onto them. They're hard to find.

CHAPTER 11
Sell your value

Only a fool thinks price and value are the same.
Antonio Machado

Few businesses can expand and grow without fresh injections of capital, so it makes sense to understand the banking landscape you're operating in and give yourself the best chance of success. I've learned a few things along the way that may help you navigate this torturous exercise.

How to choose the right bank

I can't stress how important it is to develop a good relationship with your banker and to start building that relationship before you need them and their money. While they will always crunch the numbers to assess your creditworthiness, they will also assess you as a person to decide whether or not to take a gamble on you. Whether you choose to work with a traditional bank, mutual society, credit union or national bank, you'll find their policies and procedures are similar.

For a start, choose a bank that knows your needs. This sounds obvious, but certain banks specialise in loans for certain industries. For example, our bank has a strong presence in hospitality: the bankers understand it and are (reasonably) sympathetic to the undulations of this erratic industry. Mind you, when a bank changes its CEO (and this is happening more and more frequently than in the past), the preference and risk tolerance for an industry can change along with it, so you need to keep your finger on the pulse of what's happening in your industry.

That's why joining your local association or industry advocacy body is so important. They often hold seminars or events that cover topics such as how to choose the right bank and you can ask anyone a question and get a quick answer. If you move in the right (industry) circles, you'll also discover that if a particular bank has had a bad experience with someone in your industry, they may be unwilling to work with you. Knowledge is power. Do your homework so you don't waste time chasing down deals with bankers who are never going to say 'yes'.

Once you've found the right bank, try to find the right banker to work with. The people working in the bank can differ wildly in how they value a business, assess risk, understand the cyclical nature of what you do (and so on), so if you can get a good referral from an industry insider as to who they like and work with, take that referral seriously: it could be the difference between getting approval or not. Once that's done, you'll receive a business finance agreement (or BFA), also known as a term sheet, which will contain the details of your banking covenant.

The BFA covers off things such as loan-to-value ratios (LVRs), interest rates and when payments are due, length of loan, terms and conditions, and more. It will also cover off on personal guarantees, which is something you should look at very closely because conditions like this could be used against you in the future and bring you down. I know of many successful entrepreneurs who signed off on personal guarantees and even though they made all the appropriate payments, the banks called in the loan and the entrepreneurs went bust trying to pay it off. If you start with that assumption and work backwards, it will help you manage your expectations and prevent disappointment.

You might think all this is pretty standard stuff, and it is, but the devil is in the detail and there could be clauses or conditions that are seriously unhelpful to you should things turn bad in the future. You must review these documents with your accountant and lawyer to ensure you're not signing something that could come back to bite you.

Most people never need to review any contract until the shit hits the fan, and then everyone is scrambling to find a decades-old contract that's sitting in some dusty filing cabinet somewhere, hoping and praying that they didn't sign or agree to something that's no longer in their interest to agree to. More often than not, they signed it, without reading it first, and they will suffer the consequences.

In short, don't sign anything you haven't read and understood. If you don't understand it, ask questions, and if you still don't understand it, ask more questions. It's on your head if you don't understand what you're signing.

ATTENTION BANKS: HOW TO LOSE A VALUABLE CUSTOMER

I was a very loyal customer of a bank. I will refrain from naming them as I may need them one day. We were pretty happy with the service we were getting until one particular large transaction they were financing for us. At the very last minute, despite telling us we could use a particular valuer for this transaction, they informed us that they would use a different valuer. Clearly, their word was not their bond and I have no time for people who renege on deals, verbal or otherwise. I sought out a previous banker I had worked with, who was delighted to welcome us back and we've had a wonderful relationship ever since.

I'm not the only one who's had a negative experience with a bank. A good friend of mine owned a very popular Sydney nightclub. It specialised in live entertainment and was incredibly successful. He'd been around for decades and had never missed an interest payment. After the bank revalued his business, his interest payments went up, he missed one payment and the bank forced him to sell. True story.

A bank can make or break your business. Build a relationship with them, choose one that understands your industry and take the time to get to know your business banker so that if the proverbial hits the fan, you can ring and speak to them, get it sorted and keep moving.

How to choose a good accountant

Before you start your business (yes, before you've even bought your company name, website domain name or anything else for that matter), you need to have the right accountant. This is absolutely crucial. A good accountant will assist you in building the foundation of your business, and help you set the goals and create the game plan to get you there. The good accountants offer much more than just a window to the past. The consultative accountants—the ones you want—will help you look to the future to identify what you want and plot out the pathway to help you get there.

The challenge most small-business owners have in hiring an accountant is the cost. 'I can't afford it!', 'They charge like wounded bulls' and 'They bill me for picking up the phone' are common complaints. While this may all be true, the reality is you can't afford not to have an accountant work with you. They should be seen not as an expense, but as an investment. Just as you buy a property with an expectation of a return, you should do the same with your accountant.

My accountant is one of my most trusted advisors. We meet regularly, set the goals and work hard together to achieve them. I tell her what my goals are. She helps me get there. End of story. Why wouldn't I reward her for that effort? She is available to talk and we meet whenever we need to.

Top 9 questions to ask an accountant (before you engage them)

1. Can I speak to three of your current clients?

2. What experience do you have in my sector?

3. What is your business model for working with clients?

---

4. What qualifications do you have?

5. What other firms have you worked for?

6. What services do you offer? (Do you just do basic tax preparations or do you get involved with goal setting and business planning?)

7. Will you personally do the work or will it be delegated to a junior?

8. What if we don't get along? How will we do an exit?

9. How will we do the handover to a new advisor if we terminate our arrangement?

You can use these same questions to find a good lawyer.

What not to do when choosing an accountant

While it's tempting to pick someone you know to be your accountant—your uncle, best friend, the cousin of your neighbour—don't. You want a specialist in your sector. I am in hospitality so I choose advisors who have experience in this sector.

To find a specialist in your field, join your local associations because they'll be able to put you in contact with people who have the appropriate experience. Or ask a respected colleague in your field who they use. Ask enough people and you'll find the same names will pop up. They're the advisors you want.

These same tips on how to choose an accountant can also be used to choose a lawyer, financial advisor and other advisors.

On a pleasing note, I've discovered that the most expensive firms are not always the best. Sometimes the lesser known, boutique advisory firms do a much better job, are more responsive and charge less. Don't assume that high price equals a better service. Having had some fun with lawyers, it would be remiss of me not to have some fun with accountants. And let it be said, I hold good accountants in the same high esteem as I do good lawyers. They are worth their weight in gold, and then again. Here's an interpretive guide to help you communicate with your accountant.

When they say ...	What they really mean is ...
I will just put that in an Excel.	I can't explain it to you in plain English.
Let me come back to you on that.	I don't know what you're talking about.
I can only give you advice about accounting.	I don't know anything at all about your business.
If you increase the gross profit margin by 3% you will make a lot more money.	I have no idea how a price increase will impact your customers.
You will need to pay tax on that increased profit.	I am a killjoy, have limited emotional intelligence and am not taking into account any of your hard work.
I love numbers.	I prefer being behind a desk and not communicating with anyone in the real world.

Crowdfunding: Leveraging your community to raise money

I have been raising capital for decades now and have always done it the old-fashioned way: locate a pub to buy, prepare my information memorandum, source the funds from investors or the bank and get to work. If you'd prefer to bypass the banks altogether, there are new financing alternatives you can consider.

For example, with the advent of technology, crowdfunding has become a convenient way of raising capital to fund a project and has changed the funding game completely. You've no doubt heard of the concept, but if you haven't, crowdfunding is simply a way of raising funds from a number of people over the internet to help you start a product or to help you make a profit.

Pozible was one of Australia's first crowdfunding start-ups and it helped launch a product that is close to my heart, mainly because we sell it in our pubs. Four Pillars gin distillery is a small gin distillery in the Yarra Valley, Victoria, about 90 minutes north of Melbourne. Its three founders, Cam, Matt and Stu, had worked in wine for years, and in 2013 decided to start Four Pillars with the ambition of making the best craft spirits in Australia. They turned to crowdfunding to fund the first batch of their coveted Rare Dry Gin. Four days after launch, they'd sold out of their first batch and made $10 000. They ran another campaign to fund their next batch, sold it to 306 people, made $31 200 and have never looked back.

Four Pillars showed that 'rewards' crowdfunding is a legitimate and efficient way to test, launch and sell a brand-new product and find your first customers along the way. The key advantage of this form of crowdfunding is you don't have to give any equity or shares away.

There's no two ways about it. Capital raising can be hair raising, but if you're to grow, expand and realise the full potential of your amazing business idea, you'll need to get stuck into it eventually. Whatever method you use to raise money, know that everything comes with obligation and commitment, so be sure to choose wisely, honour the agreements you commit to and don't overpromise.

Summing up ...

1. Choose an accountant who will work closely with you to help you achieve your financial goals, not one who just wants to do your tax.

2. Do your due diligence before you choose your accountant. Once you appoint one, it's expensive and time consuming to change.

3. Don't assume that a higher price equals a better service.

4. Capital raising can be hard work, but if you're going to grow and expand, you'll need to get good at it.

5. Choose a bank that understands your industry or sector. Join your industry association and ask members who they bank with.

CHAPTER 12
Sell your brand

No man is free who is not master of himself.

Epictetus

Rebranding, renovating and revaluing our pubs are the key elements to how we grow our business. It's expensive, time consuming, energy intensive and, in the short term, unlikely to create extra sales. The ROI (return on investment) on a rebrand is notoriously low for any business, but if you don't do it, you can run the risk of losing relevance with your target audience. By the time you've realised it, your target market has moved on to another venue and you face the impossible task of bringing them back. I liken bringing back a disengaged audience to turning around the *Titanic*. It can be done, but it's time consuming, hard and will have zero impact on the final outcome.

What is a rebrand?

A rebrand is when we take the pub we already have in a different direction. It could mean we reposition the pub to attract a new demographic or revive an existing pub to retain its existing customer base (and attract new people too). There are two parts to any rebrand. There's the concept development, and there's the execution. I strongly recommend you bring in outside help to conduct your rebrand. You're almost certainly too close to the business to get a bird's eye view of how others see it and getting a third party to assist you with this can be a great way to get perspective.

There are many branding 'experts' out there who will happily take your money to provide you with a mood board and a few screenshots of possible fonts and colours for your new brand and then leave you to it. Good branding experts will take the time to ask you a series of questions and do a deep dive into who you are, what you and the business stand for, what you offer, what the future looks like and how you fit into the competitive landscape. It's a mystical process in some respects and the best ones will take on board all you tell them and come back to you with a comprehensive demonstration of what your new brand could be. Will it cost you? Yes. It's not cheap so you want to make sure that you're in a position to not only afford that consultant's fee but to execute the rebrand as well. Could you do it yourself? Sure, but like room service, it tastes so much better when someone does the cooking for you.

How do you do a rebrand?

We did a rebrand for the Hunt Hospitality brand, the overarching entity that owns all our pubs. It was an eight-week process and the branding experts homed in on our 'why'. There are three key questions a branding expert will ask you to get to the heart of a rebrand:

- Who are you targeting?

- What are you offering?

- Why would they choose you?

Once that's established, the corporate colours, messaging and execution can be created. Then you need to take action to ensure it all gets executed and is done according to plan.

The 4-step plan for rebranding your business

A rebrand can get really complicated and expensive very quickly. But there are a few steps you can take to ensure it rolls out smoothly and gives you minimum headaches.

1. Get commitment and buy-in from the team

Change is confronting for most people so it pays to ensure that you communicate your vision to the team and explain your 'why' behind the rebrand so that everyone can feel safe and understand that their jobs are not at risk. This could be conducted as a 'town hall' meeting, which is a grand term for getting your team together in the one room, or via Zoom, so you can communicate the vision once for everyone to hear at the same time.

2. Identify the tasks to be completed

A rebrand could be as simple as changing the logo and your marketing collateral, which in itself is a really big job even for the smallest of operations. Just think about all the places your logo appears—each one of those pieces will need to be revised and updated.

For us, there were lots of elements that needed to be changed when we rebranded: logo, pub signage on the front of the building, website, menus, wall posters, corporate stationery, drink coasters, marketing brochures, newspaper advertising, radio advertisements, wayfinding signage, staff uniforms, TV and video advertising, logos on social media platforms—and much more.

We rebranded the entire company so we started with the website and built the messaging from there. We used a creative copywriter to express our messages, created language rules and terms in a way that would make our audience understand our big 'why' and hired a graphic designer to create the brand guidelines (the colours, fonts, camera angles and photographic shots).

Once the brand guidelines were established, we passed them on to our photographers, social media and internal marketing team to ensure the overall concept was maintained and showcased consistently across all facets of the business.

For a multi-pronged organisation like mine, a rebrand is a massive endeavour and if it gets rolled out in a slow, drip-fed way, without urgency or a time line, it can lose its momentum.

3. Choose your agency (or do it yourself)

If you're going to roll out the rebrand yourself, you need to feel confident enough to brief the creative teams to deliver the goods: directing the web developer, the photographer, the graphic designer, the copywriter, and so on. This is a task in itself and I had my marketing manager Ricci-Lee manage it all. If you don't have a person like Ricci-Lee on your team, and you know your strengths are not in marketing (and you can afford it), you can outsource it. There are a lot of freelance marketing managers available via outsourcing websites such as Upwork and Freelancer.

Canva, a free design platform, is a brilliant tool for those on a budget. You can use it to design a logo, brochures, slide decks, websites, business cards, and much more. You simply choose your layout, choose your colours and font, copy and paste your text in, press 'download' and you've got your new marketing collateral.

You can also check out digital marketing influencers on Instagram and Facebook as they give away lots of tips and tricks on how to grow your digital brand. At the end of the day, if you hire the right people, they'll be one of the best sources of word of mouth for your brand.

4. Own the strategy documents, the copyright and the codes

You must ask the branding experts to hand over the strategy document that makes all their thinking and insights tangible. Without that, the whole concept can become a 'pie in the sky' exercise: opaque to understand

and impossible to implement. The strategy document should include very clear milestones about what needs to happen so that you can action the plan without needing them to implement it for you. Of course, they can do it for you, but they'll take a clip of the ticket each time, which ends up costing you more.

Be careful with graphic designers and web designers because some will cheekily word the terms and conditions to ensure they own the copyright to your logo and web design, which means, technically, you're licensing the logo and web design from them. This may not matter in the short term but if you fall out with them for some reason and the goodwill is no longer there, they can withhold the use of that logo and web design, which could prove disastrous.

The same goes for hosting your own website, managing the website backend and content management systems, and owning the codes to your company URL name (website name). These are critical components and if you don't own and manage them, you could become hostage to a company who will withhold them from you and make you pay a sum of money to get them back. It could bring your business down, or at the very least, cost you dearly.

In short, ensure in the terms and conditions that you own all the designs, and ensure that someone on your team, or your IT person, takes responsibility for being able to access and log on to all your systems.

I often get asked whether it's worth learning how to update your own website or whether you should pay a web designer or developer to do it. My advice is to definitely learn how to update your own website. Yes, it's a pain; yes, it's outside your skillset; and yes, it's time consuming, but unless you have the budget to pay someone $80 an hour (or more) to change the tiniest of details—such as dates, times, prices, and so on—all of which change constantly on a pub website, you're going to be up for thousands of dollars a year. If you don't want to do that, hire a virtual assistant or web freelancer who can do it for you for a fraction of the cost your web developer charges.

We paid for our strategy, loved it, ensured that we got a copy of everything and executed it cost-effectively at our own pace in-house.

How do you measure the success of a rebrand?

We usually measure the success by the PR we receive. This takes work on our behalf too as we need to conduct an outreach program to tell everyone we've rebranded. This could take the form of speaking gigs, stories in the local newspaper, guest comments on TV or radio, winning awards (I recently won regional Australia's most prestigious award in our field, the Hunter Business Awards 'Business Leader of the Year' award, and we were also voted Australia and New Zealand's second-most innovative company in the hospitality, retail, tourism and entertainment sector by the *Australian Financial Review* Boss Most Innovative Companies awards, beating the Coles groups in the process).

The foundation to achieving this kind of PR is based on the fact that we are super clear on what we stand for, what we do and what our point of difference is. These three critical facts were dealt with at the start of the process and were embedded in our DNA, which in turn showed up in our logo, colours, font, imagery and words and that, of course, translates to our customers in the form of all our signage, marketing collateral, promotions, customer service and everything else.

When should you do a rebrand?

It's hard to say when you should do a rebrand, but I know when not to do a rebrand, and that's when you don't have the budget to implement it. Getting a rebrand is one thing, implementing it is another, so unless you have extra funds in your kitty to pay for the rollout, don't bother starting a rebrand.

Top 4 ways to know when you need a rebrand

1. Your design is out of date.

2. Your customer base changes.

3. Your branding colours and trimming no longer make you happy or drive you to succeed.

4. Your brand doesn't match your goals.

What will a rebrand cost?

A rebrand of one asset—that is, one pub or venue—can cost between $10000 and $20000. An overarching corporate rebrand and strategy can cost $20000–$50000 and upwards. At some point, you have to determine what the return on the investment is likely to be, how long the rebrand will last, what your vision is for the business and what percentage of sales you are happy to spend to achieve it all.

You may have to compromise on what you can get done and allocate resources effectively. For example, if you're a small business on a high street, signage will be the most important marketing tool, so invest in getting a high-quality sign and go hell for leather in using it to attract as much attention as possible.

How long should a rebrand take?

If managed correctly, a corporate strategy rebrand should take eight weeks to plan and eight weeks to execute. A rebrand of one asset could take four weeks to plan and four weeks to execute.

Promotions that have worked for us

We've had some cracker promotions over the years. One memorable one is the 'Tinny full of tinnies' promotion. We partnered with Toohey's to create a charity event where we filled an aluminium dinghy with cans of Toohey's beer and raffled it off for charity. Our target audience were beer drinkers, who lived on the coast and had young families so we hoped this promotion would fit the bill.

It did. We toured the boat to all our regional pubs, notified the media before it arrived and ensured the public knew the event was happening, so that when the boat arrived it was greeted with much fanfare and attention. The year we ran this promotion we raised $100000 for the children's charity, Variety.

In another promotion, we gave away free chicken schnitzels and had 2800 people lined up to receive them, resulting in a massive increase in bar and gaming sales.

A sample of a beer promotion we ran for one of our pubs.

Rebranding involves meetings – lots of meetings

There's a lot to manage when you take on a renovation or a rebrand. There'll be lots of people and suppliers involved and a mountain of meetings to make it all happen. If you're not careful, you'll find your time eaten up with meetings that may not be useful. Unplanned and unstructured meetings suck up everyone's time, energy and resources and mostly achieve nothing. This mainly happens because meetings are called too often or for the wrong reason. The key is to identify what decisions need to be made, and then decide if a meeting is required to make them.

Jeff Bezos, founder of Amazon, believes there are two types of decisions. If the decision is big in that the outcome is audacious, expensive or irreversible, it's a Type 1 decision and a meeting is necessary. If the decision is minor in that the outcome is inexpensive, reversible or low impact, then it's a Type 2 decision and you should empower your team to act on it without calling everyone to a meeting to discuss it.

The trouble is, as Bezos recounts, we often treat Type 2 decisions as Type 1 and resign ourselves to endless meetings and emails, depriving our organisations of speed and our people of autonomy and satisfaction. If you can distinguish between the two and empower your people to make and act on Type 2 decisions, you'll find that output and productivity will skyrocket.

Assuming you are now meeting to discuss Type 1 decisions, ensure the meeting is run with military-style precision. I run my meetings very tightly, I have clear guidelines for how they operate and I make sure everyone who attends knows the rules.

My 4-step SORT process for running successful meetings

1. **S**et up

2. **O**utline your values

3. **R**esponsibilities

4. **T**ime

Set up

- *Start on time:* don't wait for latecomers. If you do, everyone will start arriving late. Don't punish the punctual for the sins of the tardy.
- *Be prepared:* all information for a meeting must be sent to everyone two days prior so they can review it before they attend.
- *No phones:* the chit chat at the start of a meeting is invaluable for building relationships and rapport.

Outline your values

- *Be accountable:* if you make a mistake, apologise and make amends. We're all human and if you lead by example when you make a mistake, your staff are more likely to own up to theirs too.
- *Be reliable:* do what you say you are going to do. Nothing builds trust quicker than being someone people can rely on.
- *Be brave:* don't agree with a course of action or strategy because everyone else does. Stand your ground. It demonstrates to others that you value cordial dissent.

Responsibilities

- *Be clear:* set clear deadlines of who is doing what, and by when. This must be made clear at the end of the meeting so everyone has direction on what they have to do. Everyone must take their own minutes.

- *Speak up:* at the conclusion, everyone must be aware of their duties and time frames. Speak up if you're not clear, or you'll be expected to deliver on the outcomes you agreed to.
- *Be a team player:* if you don't have a better solution, be open to working with the person who suggested the idea and collaborate with them to come up with a better solution.

Time

- *Get the facts:* if you can't make a decision, ask for more time to get the information you need, and then nominate a time frame for when you'll come back to the group with an update. Don't make judgements without having the full facts to hand.
- *Be specific with outcomes and timings:* all minutes and action items must include a date, meeting intention, attendees, key decisions, tasks and ownership so that everyone is clear about who owns what.
- *Allocate 'review' time:* leave time at the end of the meeting to review and agree on the minutes so that you don't run short and people don't leave the meeting not knowing what they need to do next.

Rules of engagement

While the business owner sets the rules for how and when meetings operate, it really pays to train your team on how to participate at a meeting. Once everyone knows and embraces these values, meetings will become more productive, less combative and more enjoyable.

Here's my six-step guideline for how to participate in a meeting:

- *Be respectful:* if you have a query or questions—or you don't agree with a position—ask for clarification respectfully. For example, 'I am curious as to why ...'

- *Avoid nostalgia:* the past is not always a good measure of what will work in the future. Refer to it, learn from it, but don't let it dominate the present or be a reason why something won't work this time.

- *Be empathetic:* before making a judgement, put yourself in the shoes of the other person and see things from their point of view.

- *Seek to understand:* before commenting, communicate your understanding of the situation so you can confirm you have the facts.

- *Be optimistic:* when trying something new, hope for the best and prepare for the worst.

- *Be mindful:* don't say the first thing that comes into your head. Consider the impact, see it from all angles and know that everything you say has an impact, even those flippant, off-the-cuff remarks that get made when you think no-one is listening. These often leave a lasting impression.

Selling your brand is a critical element in helping customers (and investors) understand who you are, what you do, how you're different and why you're better. In today's competitive marketplace, it's never been more important to provide stakeholders with reasons to do business with you. Selling your brand helps you do that.

Summing up ...

1. A rebrand can be an effective way to relaunch a business and improve its capital value.

2. Choose your rebranding marketing team carefully, get clarity on what the deliverables will be and ensure you own the rights to everything they create.

3. A rebrand will take longer than you think and cost more than you think. Factor that into your plans.

4. Hiring a marketing freelancer to conduct and roll out the rebrand can be more cost effective than hiring a marketing agency.

5. Avoid unstructured meetings. Use my four-step SORT process for running a successful meeting.

Conclusion

When I started out as that four-year-old kid swapping Lego bricks with Luke; when I built that backyard beer garden with my mates; when I bought my first bar (and had to find $1 million in one day to do so), little did I know that I would go on to create a pub empire valued in excess of $100 million, employ more than 350 staff, win multiple awards, launch the careers of many other successful publicans, deliver outstanding returns to my team of loyal investors and serve more than 1.5 million customers every year. Little did I know that the pub I first managed (which came with a house attached to it) would become the share house where I would meet my girlfriend Fidelma, who would subsequently go on to become my wife and the mother of my five beautiful children, and that she would help me craft a life of fatherhood, friendship and service that would enable me to give back to my beloved communities as much as those communities have given me.

In short, pubs have given me everything. They have given me my life.

I hope your business—whatever it is that you choose to find, build and sell—can do the same for you.

Let's talk!

Stephen Hunt offers guidance and mentorship to aspiring entrepreneurs globally. To access business coaching, workshop opportunities and speaking event dates, you can find information at his website: www .stephen-hunt.com.au

If you are eager to learn more about Stephen Hunt's story, life lessons and his future endeavours, you can engage with Stephen through his social media accounts:

Facebook: @officialstephenhunt

Instagram: @officialstephenhunt

Twitter: @stephenhunt1234

Whether you're new to business building or you're a business owner in need of a pick me up, Stephen Hunt welcomes you to contact him directly at: stephen@hunthosp.com.au

Stephen Hunt is looking forward to hearing from you.

Index